SUBTLE SPIRITS

SUBTLE SPIRITS

A Handbook of Hauntings, Spirits, and Mediumship

KEITH MILLER

Contact at http://www.turtlesandcrows.com

Subtle Spirits: A handbook of hauntings, spirits, and mediumship.

Keith Miller.

ISBN: 978-1-7337688-1-8

To those who have been patient
with me that I might learn

Table of Contents

Introduction 1
Ghosts, Specters, and Spirits 3
Ghosts 4
Demons 8
Classifying Spirits 12
Wandering Spirits and Spirits of Place 12
Relative Intelligence 15
Power and Influence 16
Element 17
Origin 18
Energetic Form 20
Haunted Houses, Haunted Places 23
Houses and Homes 23
Institutions 28
Hospitals 29
Hospitality Industry 31
Libraries 33
Prisons 34
Groves, Woods, and Forests 35
Lakes, Ponds, Rivers, and Streams 39
Historical Sites, Battlefields and Sites of Trauma 40
Battlefields 41
Sites of Trauma 42
Ley Lines and Nexuses 44
Crossroads and Crypts 47
Cemeteries 47

Crossroads 50
Thresholds 52
Possessions and Personal Hauntings 55
Forceful Possession 55
Oracles 57
Personal Haunting 59
Haunted Objects 61
Ghost Hunting and Paranormal Investigations 65
An Introduction to Subtle Energy Work 77
Preliminary Exercises: Meditation and Awareness 81
Mindfulness 82
Just Noticing 84
Meditation for Energy Work 85
The Energy Body and Spirits 87
Psychometry, Imprinting, Sympathy, and Antipathy 91
Energetic Self-Defense and Self-Care 95
Self-Care 97
Shields 102
Communication via Energy 105
Clairvoyance 113
Clairvoyance via Gazing 115
Mediumship and Channeling 119
Automatic Writing 126
Talking Boards 128
Offering and Purifying 137
Offerings 137
Cleansing 140

Divination........ 143
Framing the Question........ 144
Dice Reading........ 146
Marbles in a Bowl........ 147
Pendulum Dowsing........ 147
Candle Questioning........ 150
Conducting a Session........ 153
Further Reading........ 159
About the Author........ 161

Introduction

Few things have captured the public interest so thoroughly and for so long as the investigation of the paranormal. From primitive man's first contact with spirits and the development of robust traditions of shamanism, to the high ceremonial rites of the mystery cults of the ancient world, to spiritualism, Spiritism, and the legend trips of teenagers, a fascination with the hidden world of spirits has always been part of the human experience.

For many people, this interest goes beyond casually wondering about the existence of the paranormal. People who experience hauntings often have no specific information that can help them. Those who contact paranormal investigators often get little more than confirmation that the haunting is real, but no actual solutions offered. When solutions are offered, they don't always apply.

The truth is, there are many spirits out there. Almost everywhere has some kind of spirits, be they local spirits, land-spirits, elementals or just plain ghosts. This book isn't just meant for people who are being haunted, or for paranormal investigators who regularly work with ghosts. It's not just for aspiring mediums and psychics interested in contacting the spiritual world. It's for everyone, because everyone interacts with spirits in some way.

When I set out to working on *Subtle Spirits*, I wanted to provide a tool by which people experiencing hauntings could turn the situation to their advantage, rather than just being rid of the ghost. Before I settled on *Subtle Spirits*, the working title was "the Harmonious Haunting." My hope is that everyone can learn to not just live with spirits, but to fruitfully benefit from the unseen forces that live around all of us.

In the first part of the book, I describe the most common kinds of spirits involved in hauntings in North America and Europe. I detail common locations for hauntings, why these locations are so commonly involved with the paranormal, and the spirits that are generally involved. I also discuss paranormal investigation, and how mediums can assist in them.

The second part is a brief introduction to the actual practice of mediumship—communication with spirits—through the development of intuition and psychic senses. I also discuss common methods for protecting oneself and one's environment from malicious spiritual influences. I have also included traditional non-psychic means for communicating with spirits and for protecting oneself and one's home from spiritual attack.

Ghosts, Specters, and Spirits

Before we can talk about a haunting, we must address: what *is* a haunting? How we answer this question sets the tone for our entire approach. Typically, a haunting is defined as the experience of a presence, sometimes persistent, sometimes transient, of a spirit, ghost, or otherwise otherworldly visitor. Within parapsychology, this generally refers to when these experiences are recurrent in a location; in contrast to a *poltergeist*, which is generally fixated on a person. While this is a fairly clear and concise definition, it leaves us with another problem: what are *those things*? What exactly are these spirits, ghosts, or otherworldly visitors? And the answer unfortunately varies quite a bit depending on whom you choose to ask.

There have been many answers to the question of what it is that is doing the haunting, and I think we can say with some certainty that there are a variety of beings that can haunt. Here I will use the term "spirit" as the general term for the entire class of beings that exist usually without any kind of physical form. Spirits are sentient beings themselves, which exist in some other form than we do – they are generally incorporeal, but yet they can interact in some way or another with this world (if they couldn't, we wouldn't be haunted at all!). I think it's important however to speak directly to the two culprits most commonly associated with hauntings, which have so captured the public perception as to almost always be the first suspicion: specifically, ghosts and demons. I think that the tendency to assume that there are ghosts or demons involved in any haunting comes only from the availability of information. That is, hauntings are something ghosts do, and, at least in the United States, a predominantly Christian culture inclines us to assume that any influence we don't understand is evil, and that evil influences come from demons. Not only are these the first assumption of most people, but they are also perhaps the most misunderstood.

Ghosts

There are many different ideas of what constitutes a "ghost" in the world; each culture and region will have its own ideas. In a large part of the world, perhaps the larger part, they are rarely understood in same way as in the Western world. In the United States and much of Europe, we often hold that ghosts are particularly the spirits of deceased people or animals that somehow linger on in a place. This is the basic assumption of Spiritualists, who established most of the conventions of mediumship. Spiritualists are most interested in ghosts as evidence of the survival of consciousness after death, and so the Spiritualist-trained attempts contact with the spirits of deceased persons.

The Spiritualist understanding of ghosts—that they are the remnants of a persisting soul which lingers prior to "passing on"—is far from universally accepted, however. Even within the magical community it is often held that the ghost is merely a reflection of the deceased: a last psychic imprint on the energy of a place, the side effect of an unhappy death but really not the remains of the same. Like the crater left by Wile E. Coyote falling from the cliff, it resembles the person, but nobody would claim that the crater is Wile E.; so, we often say the ghost is not the person but simply the impression left by the impact of their death. I have no contention with this idea, and in at least some cases, particularly hauntings taking place in the immediate aftermath of traumatic deaths, this is quite often exactly the situation. In the second section of this book, which covers subtle energy, we will learn about psychometry and creating imprints; the mechanism by which this takes place. I certainly find it more plausible than the idea that the soul of a person has somehow stuck around after death. I have seen the impressions the mind can leave on a place – that is, after all, what we're aiming to accomplish through magic generally – but I have never seen a soul as such.

It is perhaps this belief that a ghost is merely an impression, a pernicious relic of psychic energy left in the wake of a strongly emotional event, which leads to television ghost hunters and amateur paranormal investigators callously taunting spirits in attempts to agitate them into presenting themselves. Too often we see attempts to goad a manifestation out of a spirit, and often we see nothing at all but disappointment when it does not deliver. After all, if nothing manifested, perhaps there's no ghost at all?

But I do not find that the majority of hauntings are nothing more than psychic impressions left on the energy of a place. While this certainly *does* happen, it does not account for all—or even most—hauntings. First of all, such an impression generally dissipates fairly rapidly. Though the mind can imprint itself upon a place, and trauma or high emotionality can certainly contribute to the strength of that imprint, these imprints are in truth less like the dramatic Wile E. Coyote shaped crater and more like ripples in water after tossing in a rock, or jet contrails. They are neither detailed nor particularly enduring. Even large, dramatic impacts, like a plane crash, grow over in little time; why, then, do we expect that a person's mind might impress—without any intentionality—in a way that endures for hundreds of years? Or even tens of years! And while these impressions can be sustained for a very long time due to the reinforcement of others, this only really accounts for a very few high profile cases. It does not hold for the vast majority of hauntings, the most of which we never hear about at all.

We can generally tell whether a haunting is the result of an impression not only by the history of the site or object but also based on the behaviors of the spirits involved. Obviously, if there is a trauma or heavy psychic impression, this would indicate at least the possibility of the impression hypothesis. On the other hand, some spirits feed on this kind of energy and are attracted by it, so it's not definitive. However, one observable distinction is reactivity to people. A psychic impression is not sentient; it doesn't behave like a being but more like a recording, repeating the same emotions or manifesting the same way every time and under similar conditions. In short, impressions are consistent because they are not sentient beings, whereas many hauntings involve spirits that can respond and react to what we do, as well as take initiative, act in different ways, and so on. In at least some cases (I would argue the majority), hauntings seem to be the result of sentient beings.

This does not mean, however, that ghosts are in fact the soul once inhabiting a body now unfettered from the body. This is the claim of the Spiritualists of the 19th century Americans, as well as the Spiritists who derive their beliefs from Allan Kardec's work. Both movements are based primarily on the *survival hypothesis*, that is, that the consciousness or soul of a person persists after death. Instead, I find that such "ghosts" are *spirits*, sentient beings like humans or animals but existing without physical bodies. As sentient beings, like us all, spirits have desires and preferences, dislikes and aversions. Sometimes spirits are sophisticated intelligences on the order of humans, or higher, even. Just as often, spirits have intelligences little greater than that of animals, but still just as prone to desire and aversion. With this in mind, we can begin to understand why hauntings and so on often present the way they do, at liminal and transitional periods or when things have changed recently, such as construction work, new home ownership, or so on. Because these spirits can behave in remarkably human ways and in many cases will adapt the affectations and even identities of people, it is not surprising that the Spiritualists and Spiritists assumed them to be human spirits. But even Kardec, the founder of Spiritism, admonished that we should not believe a spirit's words without corroborating evidence, as spirits can be deceptive either through malice or ignorance.

Because spirits exist outside of physical space, their influence here is in part dependent on lunar and astrological phases. In new moons, the planetary influences are stronger, allowing spirits with strong relations to planetary intelligences and so on to exert more influence. In the full moon, we find the lunar energies much stronger, often empowering spirits to wield more influence over physical affairs. Despite the lack of physical forms, spirits do have bodies of sorts, and are affected by physical reality. They can also enjoy or dislike physically present things like incense, fire, or so on. This will be important later on as we begin looking at ways to interact with spirits and rituals for haunted places.

The ways in which spirits can manifest are diverse and dependent on the power, influence, and intelligence of the spirits in question. In some cases, such as the notorious "poltergeist," spirits can even move physical objects about. In most cases, however, it is suspected that the poltergeist phenomenon is not a spirit at all, but rather the result of a psychokinetic individual in the household unconsciously and unintentionally manipulating their surroundings, a phenomenon called *recurrent spontaneous psychokinesis* (RSPK). In cases where pubescent or teenage children are living in the house, this possibility should at the very least be considered. Nevertheless, some spirits do indeed have the ability to manifest psychokinetic effects.

Sometimes, spirits can manifest in visible forms or can make themselves present enough in an area as to be momentarily visible for whatever reason, and these are often termed "specters" or "apparitions." There is a significant amount of debate over how spirits are able to do this, or if they are able to do this at all. Much of this debate focuses on whether the spirit is actually becoming visible (as in, they are actually reflecting light) or instead simply projecting their image into the minds of those around them. Visible phenomena certainly *can* be the result of light reflecting off of a surface, but *perception* occurs in the mind, not in physical space.

In many cases, a spirit may appear to a person as real and physical while not actually manifesting a form. This is not a terribly difficult task. Our minds already are quick to make mistakes in perception, especially in conditions of low light or when we are emotionally uneasy. It is not terribly surprising to me that so many of these ghost hunting television shows so frequently fail to find video evidence of even the most pernicious and active hauntings, as it is not nearly as easy to deceive a digital camera as it is a human mind. Even film cameras found themselves subject to easy influence in the past, but the use of the most modern and technologically advanced equipment does not make the detection of the paranormal easier, but rather harder. If a spirit is only manifesting an illusion in our minds, there will be no record; and where a spirit may have been able to impress itself onto film, it is not so easy to do this with digital footage.

Specters and apparitions, poltergeists, and vague impressions of not being alone, or emotions and so on arising spontaneously, are all forms of manifestation that can be made by a variety of spirits. Whether this spirit is intelligent or not seems an exercise better explored through contact or interaction than through wild conjecture or speculation. Too often, be it because of religious ideas or just narrow thinking, we leap to conclusions. Chancing upon a purportedly haunted house, we assume because of our cultural preconceptions that it must be by spirits of the dead. Unless, of course, we are of a particular religious bent. In that case, people tend instead to jump to a different conclusion: demons.

Demons

The word "demon" has been through quite the evolution through time, but with the Christianization of the West we have settled uneasily on the idea that a demon is an evil spirit, one that may or may not be of Hell, and which is haunting a place, or a person, for reasons unknown, but *not good ones*. Far be it from the spirits of the Greeks, the *eudaimones* that later became the muses of artists. With the dominance of monotheism, and the strict dualism that goes with it, we tend to believe that either a spirit must be angelic, or of God, or it must be demonic.

My objection to this hasty characterization is first that it is extremely culturally biased. The idea that spirits must be either followers of the Christian god or followers of evil doesn't give much hope at all for the numerous spirits of other religions or other regions of earth. It hardly seems fair to characterize a Tibetan land-owning spirit (*sa-dag*) as evil merely because it does not follow the Abrahamic faith at all. I think it's fair to say generally that we would not do the same for people. Reasoning people tend generally to at least give adherents of other faiths the benefit of the doubt that they are not *evil*, and I see no reason not to afford spirits the same benefit. Simply because a spirit doesn't work for the god or goddess of your choice is no reason to label it a demon.

When it is not for doctrinal reasons, we often tend to label any seemingly malevolent actors as demons. Still, I don't find this a useful classification either. For example, we first have to look at the actual motivation of an action to determine if it is really malevolent at all. Most people, at least in the US today, do not fault the landlord for collecting rent, or the banker for collecting interest, but a spirit that tried the same would almost surely be considered evil. We don't hold any ill will to territorial wild animals when we wander into their lands, either, and surely don't consider them *evil*. Ignorant, at worst, and in some cases even noble. We often hold a person at fault when they, through ignorance or stupidity, find themselves bitten by the snake or eaten by the mother bear, but when the human falls to harm from a spirit, it's suddenly an agent of the Dark Lord himself.

This tradition is not born of a vacuum, nor is it a modern occurrence. Since at least the 1100s, "demon" has been a term used for spirits that are not primarily servants of the Christian god, at least occasionally. Early grimoires which speak in some depth on binding demons and forcing them to one's will commonly follow this pattern. The Key of Solomon, for example, discusses the binding of demons and even does so in the sense of these being evil spirits, bound by Solomon in the *goetia* that lends its title to an entire branch of ceremonial magic. *Goetia* is contrasted with *theurgy* in that the latter involves the conjuration and commanding of angels or Christian spirits, whereas the former focuses on non-Christian or demonic entities.

There are certainly malevolent spirits in the world; spirits which due to jealousy, anger, or other afflictive emotions, see fit to do us harm. And why shouldn't there be? There are also malevolent people who through their own afflictive emotions wish to harm others. These spirits are sometimes born from the commission of murders or other heinous crimes, and by the deaths of those who commit such actions. But I do not find the distinction or term "demon" particularly useful when looking at the source of a haunting. Again, it seems best to use the generic term "spirit," and we can elaborate on that if it means us harm by calling it "unfriendly." This is in contrast with the already clear "friendly" spirits, whose presence many people would not even consider haunting. The ancestral spirits and protectors of our family lineages for generations, the household spirits and land spirits that have watched over our homes, we rarely hear of these in the context of "hauntings" because the beneficiaries have nothing to complain about or report. Then, too, there are many ambivalent spirits who simply do not care at all for the physical goings on around them. We generally ignore these as well; they don't have much to say, and usually only a few sensitive individuals even know they are there. We end up with so many reports of unfriendly spirits mostly out of a sampling error.

In addition to "friendly" or "unfriendly," another useful dichotomy for spirits is that of "wrathful" versus "peaceful" dispositions. This distinction comes from Tibet, though as a classification we can apply it to any spirit. Wrathful spirits are certainly more likely to make themselves known and to make demands. Peaceful spirits are generally more tolerant, and even if unhappy are more likely to avoid conflict than to engage in it. Indeed, it is in part my goal to encourage everyone in the psychic and magical communities to behave more like peaceful spirits ourselves. Far too often I see beginning sorcerers jump immediately to the most wrathful course of action. Upon finding the spirits one cohabitates with unhappy, the beginning sorcerer immediately prepares for the banishing, for the eviction notice, without trying to smooth things over first. The distressed family brings the local priest for the exorcism. If you take nothing else from this book, I hope it is that we should consider spirits not unlike other human beings. Spirits, too, have thoughts, feelings, likes, and dislikes, and if a spirit is making itself known for some reason or another, it is more likely to be fruitful to investigate *why* than simply to chase it away.

In summary, I do not find the classifications of "ghosts" or "demons" particularly useful, "specters" are merely a form of presentation of spirits, and all of these can broadly be grouped as spirits. In at least some cases, but not most cases, the haunting may simply be a significant psychological impression made upon the energy of a place. In most cases, some form of spirit exists, but that spirit's motivations and intelligence are unknown without further investigation. What might we expect to find, however, with that investigation?

Classifying Spirits

The classification of spirits is a subject which has had entire grimoires and texts dedicated to it[1]; and summarizing these would be an extensive effort deserving of its own book, rather than a part of a chapter. Focusing instead on the kinds of spirits commonly involved in hauntings, however, things become much more manageable. For the sake of completion, and because it is not unlikely that some readers may practice mediumship as described in the second part of this book in areas not traditionally considered haunted, and yet still find themselves successful, I will not limit myself to discussion of only "unfriendly" type spirits that much more readily come to mind. Instead, I will point out that all of these following spirits can be friendly, unfriendly, or simply ambivalent. It will be the goal of later chapters to discuss cultivating friendships, propitiating unfriendliness, and winning over ambivalence.

Wandering Spirits and Spirits of Place

Broadly speaking, we can classify spirits as *wandering spirits* and *spirits of place*. Wandering spirits, as they are termed, are not bound to nor do they occupy particular locations exclusively. Instead, they wander about here and there, without a particular home. They may be enticed to stay in places, and over enough time, may become spirits of place, but generally they roam. Typically, when wandering spirits are haunting a place, it is because something there has attracted them. Wandering spirits may be mistaken for spirits of place, and in fact the distinction becomes blurry, in the case of spirits like *decay eaters*, which feed on the energy of decay. These spirits are often found in cemeteries, nursing homes, slaughterhouses, or similar. Similarly, *smell eaters* are a class of spirits that enjoy

---

[1] Examples include the 1563 *Book of the Offices of Spirits* and the 1641 *Lesser Key of Solomon* looking at Goetia, the 1531 *Three Books of Occult Philosophy* considering elementals and astrological spirits, or more modern books like Allan Kardec's *The Spirits' Book*.

certain smells, and may be attracted to areas of heavy scents.[2] Indeed, many spirits without any kind of particular classification may wander about when they like particular things or even beings. It is not unheard of, though perhaps not very common outside the magical community, for spirits to take a liking to particular people. Spirits that do might be called "guardian angels," "protector spirits," "familiars" and the like. Because they focus around a particular person, they are not wandering spirits, though they can become wandering spirits if the person they are bound to passes on with no provision for being found again.

Spirits have likes and dislikes, and will travel to places they like, and leave places they dislike. While some spirits, such as decay eaters, move about based on necessity, others need very little, and are instead driven by a desire to be around the things they enjoy. Such spirits may be attracted to aesthetics of any sort, to the energy of a place, or even to ideas and concepts, finding their home near people who think similarly to themselves. These are less likely to be vocal, and so may be unknown cohabitants. Happy spirits rarely make for bad housemates, and so as such may not attract any attention at all. On the other hand, unhappy spirits are unfriendly spirits, which as we've already discussed make up the majority (though not all) of the kinds of hauntings that disturb people enough to consider that they may, in fact, be in a haunted place.

Spirits of place, on the other hand, are intrinsically bound to a particular place. The aforementioned land-owning spirits are an example, being aptly named as spirits that rule

---

[2] Decay eaters and smell eaters are part of an Eastern classification of spirits. They are not a particular kind of spirit so much as a way for us to classify them; there are many different "types" of smell eaters and decay eaters, all grouped together by what they eat. Something like saying "herbivores," where many different animals can be herbivores.

over certain geographical locations. Similarly, the tree spirits and spirits of groves, creeks, hills, mountains, and so on recognized commonly by druids or shamanic and animistic cultures are spirits of place. The concept of spirits of place is found in cultures around the world, from the ancient Roman *genius loci* to the abovementioned Tibetan examples to the spirits of the land of Native American traditions and so on. In a much broader scale, the different and distinct deities said to rule over larger areas, tribes, or nations are a large and obvious example of a spirit of place. Family spirits and household protectors would also likely fall under the idea of a spirit of place, although generally attached to a person rather than a location particularly.

Typically, spirits of place will be happy so long as the place is undisturbed. They may be made unhappy by making significant alterations to a place. My own household spirits were unhappy when I installed solar panels; not because they didn't want the solar panels, but because I didn't consult them at all first, and the alteration required conduit running through the yard. I had a number of electronics malfunctions until these spirits were propitiated. Spirits of place may also be upset when a family moves away and a new one moves in. Many spirits are much longer lived than humans, and have little interest in the legal ownership of a property. Still, significant changes can be displeasing.

In other cases, spirits of place can become upset not from being disturbed but instead from being ignored. In Asia, people often make offerings to their local spirits. Even smaller spirits with little influence are made offerings to prevent harm. These spirits gain influence over time, but they also become used to the free meal, as it were. When this free meal no longer comes, for some time, the spirit may become upset and try to get the attention of the locals. Eventually, such a spirit will likely move on if it is able, or otherwise will go into a kind of hibernation, or die.

We cannot expect spirits accustomed to receiving offerings to stay when they stop coming, and it is possible that through the habits and unconscious rituals of previous occupants that spirits wish for simple offerings they are no longer receiving. The drinking man who always poured out the stale, unfinished bottle of beer in the yard in the morning, was making an offering without realizing it, but upon his departure the spirits realize when they aren't getting theirs. Without making an effort, it is often very difficult to determine what has upset local spirits or attracted wandering spirits, but with mediumship or divination it can be done.

Relative Intelligence

We can also classify spirits based on their relative intelligence. As mentioned before, spirits can range from the intelligence of animals to intelligence far surpassing that of humans. They may also have access to other senses. Spirits are more attuned to energetic things than people are, for example, but may be less aware of physical changes that don't effect the energetic environment as much. Like birds, the activities of spirits can portend changes or indicate environmental issues long before we recognize them. More intelligent spirits may have more sophisticated motivations, justifications, rationales, and reasons for doing what they do or liking what they like. Less intelligent spirits may be easily propitiated with a meal and strong drink left in the basement, more intelligent spirits often have the desire to communicate, to be heard. These spirits may be of the more vocal and visible variety, far more likely to make themselves known.

Many beginning psychics encounter less intelligent spirits in their first attempts to contact the spirit world, often mistaking these for evil creatures because they draw energy off of the living. It does not occur to them that this is a thing that has been happening all along, and is quite normal. Having these kinds of less intelligent spirits around is a usual thing, like having ants in a yard. It is uncommon for unintelligent spirits to wield any significant power or influence, the third way we can classify spirits.

Power and Influence

The capabilities of spirits range with the numbers of spirits, from those we might call gods or demigods that know little opposition in their dealings with mortals, to those that vary within a more fathomable scale, to the weak and powerless spirits who are more at our mercy than we are at theirs. Within the human world there is a huge range of influence and power from the prince to the pauper, and it is no different with spirits. While it would be uncommon for a god or demigod to take a very small area like a single house or room[3], such is not the case for other spirits. As a basic rule of thumb, we can say that the more spectacular the displays involved in a haunting, or the larger the area that is being haunted, the greater the collective power or influence of the spirits involved. The influence of the spirits informs us what benefits we can expect if we establish harmonious relations, and what kind of opposition we might find if we do not. It may also tell us when it may be better to simply cut our losses. It should be kept in mind however that power and intelligence are not always strongly related. While animal-like spirits may not wield the concentrated influence of the more intelligent spirits, the relative intelligence of a spirit does not correlate entirely with power. Just as there can be idiot princes and genius paupers, we can find this, too, among spirits. In any case, I do not suggest to always rely on the forceful approach of the Solomonic grimoire ceremonialist when instead we can live peacefully through the hand of friendship. In some

---

[3] This is not to say gods and demigods do not claim regions and everything within those regions. It is uncommon for a deity to claim a domain in a single object, however.

cases, it is better to live with a spirit and simply make the offerings it desires than to try to chase it away. Remember that a spirit which has the power and influence to coerce an offering out of you will also be able to wield that power and influence towards your mutual goals when the time comes.

As previously mentioned in the discussion of ghosts, it is not always uncommon for spirits to act as though they *were* spirits of the deceased. This is particularly common and often the case when the body of prevailing lore and beliefs of people encourage them to think that way. One prominent example is that of battlefield ghosts, spirits that present themselves on large battlefields. Earlier I mentioned that it would be uncommon for a single person to create a significant impression on a place that would last for very long. On battlefields, it is not a single person but a great mass of people that create an impression of misery, fear, and suffering. This oppressive aura of the battle can persist for some time, though any recent visitor to Gettysburg can attest that the spirit of that great battle is only prominent at particular times of year and phases of the lunar cycle, and most people will only sense it at night. Some of the local spirits were present at the battle, others have come and gone with time. Given the expectations of the visitors, and the general atmosphere of the place, it's not surprising that these spirits are often associated with the battle, and despite the sands of time covering over the battle, it still echoes through history to influence today.

Element

It is also possible to discuss ghosts in terms of their elemental natures. All beings are comprised of the classical elements in some configuration or another. This is not really pertinent so much to whether or not a spirit is inclined to haunt, but has implications when we are considering their preferred environments. We are more likely to find fire spirits in environments with elemental fire, watery spirits in places with water, and so on. Some spirits may have all of the classical elements as part of their energetic anatomy, but unlike physical beings with physical bodies, not every element will necessarily be represented. *Generally* wandering spirits will tend to be more attuned to fire and air, whereas spirits of place will be more attuned to earth and water, particularly the elements of their homes. Spirits, like people, can be deficient in certain elements which leads them to seek those elements out, and this naturally has implications when dealing with them.

Origin

Finally, we can classify spirits through the circumstances that lead to their creation. It is a Buddhist belief that all sentient beings upon their death are reborn into a new life, based on the causes and conditions they have cultivated or created while alive. Whether you believe in rebirth or not, the law of cause and effect is important in understanding spirits. Specifically, spirits born of positive and virtuous causes and conditions will tend towards being virtuous, compassionate, kind, and so on. Spirits born from the causes and conditions of non-virtue or immorality will be more inclined towards non-virtue. Here, the idea of "demons" makes some sense. When spirits are born out of evil actions, through the cause of the death of a murderer, rapist, particularly greedy person, or so on, we might classify this spirit as a demon. In particular, demons could be considered to be spirits that are embodiments of anger and hatred. These spirits will not be inclined towards kindness and virtue regardless, and may require more forceful means, or simply to not to be interacted with beyond making some offerings with a request to leave one alone. These spirits can be pacified, but there are no guarantees that regular magical practitioners can do this, as those with the ability to pacify "evil" spirits are usually very powerful beings who likely have no need for this book.

These kinds of spirits often tend to be born in regions associated with the being which died and created for the cause of their birth. The homes of terrible criminals, black magicians, and the like may become the haunts of the reborn spirit of that person. That said, this is not a very common outcome, and it shouldn't be the initial assumption. It is possible in the case of particularly "evil" spirits or demons in historical places, but not so much so that we should start there.

Throughout this chapter, and throughout the rest of this book, I speak of spirits in strongly anthropomorphic terms, as beings with bodies, but this is perhaps a major misconception I should put to rest now. Spirits may or may not have concrete physical forms or elemental or material forms with traditional boundaries, and though I speak of spirits as sentient beings and personalities, I do not wish to create the impression that the personal spirit, the spirit with personhood and a unique identity, is the only kind of spirit or that all spirits possess those characteristics.

The idea of a spirit of place is such that the spirit co-emerges from the place. We cannot easily separate spirit from place or place from spirit, or see where one begins or one ends, just as we cannot separate our own subtle bodies from our physical bodies. Similarly, spirits of *ideas* or *concepts* cannot always easily be separated from the idea or concept itself. Spirits of transition or liminality for example exist in those places or circumstances or situations, but whether they exist as cognitive constructs or as actual spirits is debatable. In truth, it does not matter. When we experience things as spirits, then there *are* spirits, as it is the human experience here that really matters.

The existence of spirits as constructs of the mind alone is a concept not without merit. Still, while this must be acknowledged, the identification of spirits, ghosts, demons, and so on as mere projections of mind is not useful for our purposes in this book. While we can look at spirits, indeed all sentient beings, including ourselves, as merely spontaneously arisen concepts of mind which do not exist in a concrete or conventionally real sense, and while we should look at them this way within certain spiritual practices, it does not benefit us or others to simply dismiss experiences as empty or spirits as manifestations of the mind. A spirit that represents an obstacle and is personified as a demon can and should be seen in *both* ways, at least until we're able to move beyond its conventional nature. Let us endeavor to achieve that, but for the purposes of this book, I will discuss ghosts, spirits, and so on as conventionally real and in personified terms as sentient beings, not because it's ultimately true, but because it's expedient towards our purposes.

Energetic Form

The human being is comprised not only by a physical body, but also by an etheric and astral body. Each body corresponds to a different part of the person's lived experience. The physical body obviously exists in the material world. The etheric body corresponds to the physical body. The astral body corresponds to emotions, thoughts, ideas, concepts, and awareness. Anything that enters our consciousness is represented in some form within the astral body. The etheric body is denser, as it's correlated to physical things and so strongly anchored; meanwhile, the astral body is extremely subtle, changing easily and often, just as our minds do. On the other hand, the etheric body has a limited form and is somewhat bound by spatial dimensionality; while the astral body has no such limitations and exists essentially outside the limitations of space.

Spirits, too, come in differing forms and densities. An astral spirit may be vast and expansive, encompassing huge regions and yet not being located there at all unless it chooses to be. Meanwhile, etheric spirits exist within space. Though that space corresponds to the physical world, the etheric spirit has no physical form.

In many ways, this mirrors power and influence and relative intelligence. Astral spirits are often far more expansive and of much greater intelligence. Their consciousnesses are vast and so their awareness extends over a large area. Their ability to perceive pathways by which they can exert influence to bring about physical results is also great. However, this astral body is distant from the physical world, and so they may not think in terms of normal human timeframes. Additionally, they may see great value in having physical people to affect changes on their behalf. In particularly great cases, these powerful astral beings are considered to be local gods.

Etheric beings, on the other hand, are far more connected to our world. They have dense energetic bodies comprised of highly patterned etheric energy. This energy is sometimes, though not always, anchored to physical objects which allows it to maintain its form more easily. These spirits can affect the physical world if they know how exert etheric influence onto objects, though the effects may be fairly limited or else exhausting for the spirit. Because their bodies are more connected to the etheric world than the astral, they work on a more normal timeframe. However, they tend to be less capable of exerting the powerful generational influence of astral beings.

Astral beings can create an etheric form when they need to interact acutely. In many cases, they will possess animals or other inhabitants of their domain for the purpose of interacting physically with the world. In other cases, they will make arrangements with human beings to carry out their work, in exchange for favors. Etheric beings also have astral forms, thought they are usually far more limited than those of an astral being. Like us, etheric beings have a consciousness, and so have astral bodies. However, also like us, their awarenesses are generally somewhat limited to the areas around them. They generally do not have the expansive consciousness of an astral being, a demigod or god, or of a human yogi or highly achieved master. Instead, their awareness is generally limited in scope, and they cannot see the paths to achieve the same influence as astral beings.

Haunted Houses, Haunted Places

In the previous chapter I discussed spirits, and we covered how their motivations, likes, and dislikes can lead them around. Now, we should discuss the second component of any haunting: the haunt. Generally speaking, a haunting takes place in a location, though sometimes hauntings are associated with particular people or with objects, both of which we will cover in another chapter. Hauntings can obviously take place in homes, but also any number of other locations which may or may not have any kind of particular significance. It is generally accepted that crossroads and cemeteries are often hotbeds of paranormal activity, and we will discuss these in their own chapter as well. In this chapter, we will look at folk lore and experiences of haunted places. We will also look at the kinds of spirits that are commonly attracted to different kinds of places.

Often, as was discussed in the previous chapter, the term "haunting" has a negative connotation. This is a common use that I will generally go with, but it isn't the only situation. There are certainly situations where spirits inhabit a place and are positive and beneficial. Achieving a harmonious haunting, after all, means turning negative experiences with unfriendly spirits into positive experiences with friendly spirits. This ignores that in many cases, there are already friendly spirits in a place. These friendly spirits will also be discussed in relation to their common locations.

Houses and Homes

It's likely no other kind of haunting has drawn quite as much attention as the haunted house. Whether it is due to the fact that we live and stay in our homes that has made this so prominent, the deep psychological impact of the feeling of not really owning one's own home, or the general impact of being afraid of the place where we should feel safest, the impact of the haunted house on the field of paranormal investigation and society in general cannot be denied. Unfortunately, the cause of a house haunting can also be one of the harder to determine. Whereas we'll see later that the underlying causes of a haunting in institutions or geographical features are usually fairly simple, the haunted house is not necessarily merely one or two possibilities.

Unlike in the cartoons and movies, a haunted house rarely broadcasts itself. While it's popularly the case in TV shows that a house has been haunted for the previous however many owners, haunted houses are rarely multi-generational affairs. When they are, it's usually because the story and the history cause us to broadcast and project onto the haunted house, in essence calling to the kinds of spirits that enjoy that kind of thing. Spirits exist which feed on emotions, and fear is both easy and convenient to cause. This will be discussed later when talking about historical sites and sites of trauma. In many cases where a house becomes haunted only because we believe it to be haunted, we are either imprinting onto the energy of the house, or summoning spirits through our actions. The spirit is there because we have created conditions that call to it, and it has helpfully obliged.

The typical house haunting is one or a few spirits who have either been there for a long time, or have recently been attracted by something, and who now are not having their needs or desires met. The ages-old Chick tract schtick of a child with a Ouija board opening a gateway to the other world is not *entirely* without merit, as an attempt to call to or make contact with spirits is something they tend to be attracted to. The mere act of using a talking board or the like also tends to cause us to look for things we might not otherwise have noticed at all. Where we believe new spirits are turning up, in fact we're just looking more closely for things that have been happening all along. Or, by the act of our looking we've given the impression that we'd like to communicate and the spirits are obliging us. While such amateurish attempts at contacting spirits do not usually result in demonic possession or the summoning of eldritch horrors or so on, they certainly *can* serve as an impetus for hauntings.

Similarly, offerings that are left out too long as part of regular religious practice can attract spirits. In Southeast Asia it is believed that ghosts can be attracted to left over water in offering bowls after the offerings are taken down, or if the offerings are left up overnight. Notably, in most of Asia the term "ghost" rarely refers to the spirits of the deceased, but rather to a sophisticated taxonomy of various spirits. These spirits may appear to haunt a house whenever new religious rituals are being practiced, or when changes in the house or household occur.

The most commonly reported haunted house is one where household spirits are unhappy. A great number of traditions speak of various household spirits: brownies and kobolds in Germanic cultures, the spirits inhabiting fireplaces and water sources in the East, leprechauns, some fairies, all of these refer to domestic spirits that usually get along sympathetically with the homeowner. Today, fireplace spirits and the like can be found inhabiting stovetops and ovens, and water spirits inhabiting wells and bathrooms. These spirits, when utterly neglected, can become angry, but often simply using the appliances is enough to keep these spirits happy. Still, in some cultures it's considered best to leave some food on the stove for the spirit that inhabits it after cooking meals, particularly culturally significant meals. Fireplaces, too, can be inhabited by spirits that feed on or inhabit fire. For example, when a fireplace is disused, replaced with electric or gas heat, for example, this can upset the fireplace spirit; so leaving some symbolic essence of fire in a disused fireplace is a good practice.

The two most visible kinds of hauntings in the strictly negative sense of the word are poltergeists and apparitions. Apparitions, or specters, occur when a spirit is manifesting visibly in some kind of form. Perhaps most jarringly common are human sized and shaped apparitions, as these are much more noticeable. Smaller apparitions, movements from the corner of the eye, and things like this may be dismissed as mistakes of perception, or having seen an animal or a mote of dust. While some spirits have a preference for appearing as certain animals or shapes, these are unlikely to show up inside a house. So we find that most apparitions that people *notice* are those of human sized shapes, often in windows or other places where they can use a trick of the light to make themselves known. Manifesting a physical form is not only difficult for spirits, but *exhausting*, so instead it is far more common for them to use fog, light, or other things to momentarily appear in a way we can see them. Again, the reasons for this may vary from spirit to spirit, and we will study more about how to divine their intent in a later chapter.

The word *poltergeist* means "noisy ghost" in German. These are most commonly one of two things: either a spirit which is communicating through moving objects as it knows this will get our attention, regardless of the considerable difficulty this can cause a spirit, or a person in the house manifesting psychokinetic phenomena. The latter, called *recurrent spontaneous psychokinesis*, is stereotypically a teenager undergoing some considerable stress, and manifesting these things unwittingly[4]. However, psychokinetic events can be caused by people of any age, and sometimes wittingly as well as unwittingly. When adults manifest psychokinetic phenomena, it is likely to be part of a pattern of psychic behavior that has followed them throughout their life. For children, it may be a

---

[4] A typical example of a poltergeist of this form is the Rosenheim Poltergeist, an alleged haunting in a legal office in Bavaria in the late 1960s. Investigation by German parapsychologist Hans Bender determined this to be the result of stress causing a 19 year old secretary to manifest psychokinetic activity.

first time thing, and it is important to follow up on it. We should not assume that because a child is demonstrating psychic abilities there must be a spirit in play, perhaps a possession or the like. Indeed, psychic abilities do not occur *because* of spirits but frequently they can lead to *contact with* spirits. So, when we look at a poltergeist, it is important first to rule out human causes, even if those human causes are not doing so intentionally. Today, most paranormal investigators assume that legitimate poltergeists are RSPK, and this is ruled out before continuing the investigation. Naturally, the possibility that the poltergeist is fraud or mischief is the first assumption.

Prior to this, Allan Kardec asserted that poltergeist activity was the result of spirits of low intelligence. In Kardec's model, less intelligent spirits of low morals constantly interjected into the lives of living people with disruptive activity. In the Spiritist model, these would include elementals such as sylphs, undines, salamanders, and gnomes, as well as kobolds and other domestic spirits.

The experiences of haunted houses tend to fall into a few standard categories. The hearing of sounds, usually knocking, rattling, or like someone walking; the spotting of ghostly figures, often children; the hearing of whispered voices. Just as commonly, balls of light, shadows "misbehaving," or subjective feelings of temperature changes and so on. Almost universally these couple with a feeling of someone being there, or being watched, sometimes along with an unsettling feeling or feeling of dread or fear. For these feelings of dread or fear it is actually quite difficult to determine if this is because of the influence of the spirit, or merely because of our natural reactions to something feeling "off." It is natural for us to feel unsettled if things do not quite match with our expectations. We often will have this feeling of unease in low light conditions in unfamiliar places like basements or attics, especially if we're already expecting a haunting or already have been set off by an unexpected feeling of someone present.

However, sometimes these feelings are an attempt at communication. Many spirits communicate with us telepathically, and inducing an emotion is an absolutely trivial telepathic task for most spirits unless a person is deliberately defending against it. The spirit's induction of feelings can give us some clue as to what they are trying to communicate. For example, if a spirit is inducing dread, it is likely they want us to leave. We can safely assume that it is worth looking into things further before things escalate. In the context of a house, these kinds of things can often come from renovations, changes to the family, or changes of inhabitants. Even simple changes like adding solar power or remodeling a room can be enough to upset spirits who have inhabited the home for a long time. We may think that because the spirits exist in an energetic form rather than physical form, physical changes in a room are not a big deal. However, physical changes in a room do change how the energies of a room flow, and they can change the energetic "reflection" of the room in the planes that spirits inhabit. Therefore, it is my experience that the vast majority of haunted houses are the result of normally copacetic spirits now upset by something that has been done to upset the energies of the place they call their home.

Institutions

Other than haunted houses, which rarely gain much renown except in extreme cases as they usually only receive exposure from the owners, institutions are probably the most commonly accepted haunted locations. This includes businesses, hospitals, university buildings, government offices, and other public locations where many people frequently come and go. Usually, but not always, these overlap significantly with historical locations and locations associated with traumatic events. The haunted institution may or may not be a notorious historical site. Rather, the types of activities and the subtle energies found at the location are the main factors in determining if a haunting is likely. As with houses, no single thing is predictive of haunting, but rather a variety of things coming together. Unlike houses, however, the nature of an institution itself can yield clues as to the types of spirits and their agendas.

Hospitals

Hospitals, for example, are frequently haunted locations, as are mortuaries, medical schools, and so on. Older psychiatric hospitals in particular have a reputation for being haunted[5]. In the past, psychiatric treatment was far less refined than it is today, and the degree of suffering and unhappiness was certainly attractive to both spirits who feed on that kind of suffering and spirits who desire to heal that kind of suffering. Beyond that, psychiatric hospitals are filled with psychiatric patients. This leads to the complication that mental illness is not exclusive of psychic sensitivity and often there is a great deal of overlap. It is entirely possible for a patient to be both psychic *and* mentally ill, although tragically this possibility is often overlooked due to biases of the medical community. These biases are not malicious—certainly mentally ill people can also psychotically believe themselves psychic, but it is unfortunate.

However, the situation is complicated all the more as psychotic hallucination makes it all the easier for spirits to manifest for that person. After all, the trick to manifestation is often to create a perception without actually influencing visible light, and this can be accomplished simply by influencing the mind of the intended perceiver. In cases where a person *already*

---

[5] One example of this of which I have personal knowledge is the Ridges in Athens, Ohio. This psychiatric hospital now belongs to Ohio University and most of it has been converted into administrative offices. The tuberculosis ward remains unrestored, though it is closed to the public.

has a tendency to see what is not physically there, it is that much easier to induce such a vision through telepathy. It would also be a glaring omission for me not to mention the speculative history of shamans and mediums of old being a special role assigned by a community to a person who is not entirely neurotypical.

Without making moralistic judgements on mental illness, and speaking delicately as not to imply either that psychic phenomena is all resultant of mental illness, or to imply that all cases of mental illness are actually psychics, I think it is fair to say that we must consider the lived experience of individuals, and their own reality, as the framework from which we must work in the pursuit of the study of the occult, just as we must do so within the study of psychology. Anything other than the acceptance of a person's experience of reality as *real to them* is a troubling kind of mental imperialism, where one's own experience is valued higher than that of others. With this in mind, the haunting of the psychiatric hospital can become more likely simply because they bring together people who are potentially more readily able to communicate with spirits, to say nothing of the force of projective will that the mentally ill can harness. Just because they have a mental illness does not mean their mind does not function magically in a way that might attract or evoke spirits.

So, in many cases in the case of psychiatric hospitals and facilities we must look at the idea that spirits are often attracted to these kinds of potential vectors. In the East, it is sometimes believed that spirits are likely the *cause* of the mental disease. Beyond that, thoughts and perceptions have power, and we cannot ignore the projection of certain states onto the world around them. People with psychiatric disorders who are hospitalized are often in very dark places in their lives, almost always fearful and suffering, and their projection of that fear and suffering creates a sort of dark energy which imprints onto their surroundings.

Psychiatric facilities often present a kind of institutional cheerfulness or sterility upon which the mind easily projects, and the charm of bright and childlike drawings contrasted with the suffering and sadness can create the sense of unease and dread that often indicates a haunting all on its own. Spirits, too, can be attracted to this kind of thing. As mentioned before, many spirits feed on particular kinds of emotion: suffering, unhappiness, and things like this. Once again, a hospital easily becomes a feeding ground for spirits attracted to this kind of suffering, and the vulnerability of the people within becomes a way for them to cultivate and ensure a steady supply. For a spirit that thrives on negativity and suffering, a hospital where we gather those who have a disposition to this suffering can become an irresistible place to stay.

Hospitality Industry

Bars, restaurants, and hotels are also institutions prone to haunting. In the case of bars and restaurants, the reason may be as simple as that some classes of spirits enjoy consuming the essence of liquor and alcohol. Spilled drinks are feasts for spirits, especially outside or when not cleaned up quickly. The offering of strong spirits to otherworldly beings is found across cultures, and it's no surprise. Bars and restaurants are also locations where people can spend a great deal of their lives in socialization and which people might attach to strongly. When they pass on, they can imprint heavily on the location and leave something of themselves behind. Bars in particular also represent places where many suffering people go. The wide range of emotional experiences, amplified by the easiness of drink, can be a feast for certain spirits.

Due to the rapid and frequent turnover of residents it can be difficult to know what might have been done in a hotel that could cause a spiritual incursion, but this uncertainty does not change the result. Not only that, but because hotels are often inhabited by a wide variety of people over time, a wide variety of spirits may be attracted to hotels simply to wait until their own needs or likes are met by passers through. Historic hotels in particular often accumulate stories and speculation about the identities of their ghosts or spirits. Whether that speculation is ever accurate I cannot say, I am reluctant to accept that a spirit is a human soul that has passed on; but it is not impossible for a deceased human to be reborn as a spirit that haunts a location. A spirit that finds it gets attention or becomes the subject of "ghost hunts" or paranormal investigations may happily adopt an identity over time, and may or may not actually come to believe it itself. Consider that spirits are much more sensitive to the energy we project and the ideas we hold, and that the centuries old practice of the "ghost hunt" is itself a kind of worship for that spirit, and I do not find it at all surprising that these spirits stick around in places where they have gained some fame or notoriety, and engage in behaviors that encourage it.

Schools, especially universities, also tend to become places of haunting both because of the common tendency for students to dabble in the occult as well as the long history and the variety of people passing through. Boarding schools and colleges with dormitories are particularly prone to haunting. Many spirits simply *like* studying and learning, becoming patrons of departments or patrons of certain studies or endeavors, and protectors or discouragers of certain studies or practices. In Southeast Asia some students maintain a rich spiritual life, requesting the support of deities for aiding study and passing tests. Here in the West, we do not commonly do so *directly*, but many students frequently pray for their own success on tests, and not all of these students are Christian. There are spirits that support study and can answer these prayers, and spirits that create obstacles and obstructions to study.

Students commonly find themselves going through life transitions in college. It is a place of change and liminality, transformation from the unskilled child to the skilled adult, from the unlearned layperson to the learned expert, and these transitions are attractive to spirits who live in these liminal spaces. The spirits of change and transformation are obviously attracted to the university.

In primary, elementary, and high schools we can also find hauntings, but it is my experience that in these cases the kinds of spirits that are attracted are not the kind that will stick around at the school itself. Generally, these spirits are attracted to children, transitions, and liminality. Some are attracted to the kinds of suffering and traumas that are unique to children. These spirits can be beneficial or harmful, presenting as obstacles or obstructions. They do tend to attach themselves, in my experience, to children with predispositions to the occult or esoteric, especially psychic and sensitive children. Pertinent particularly to schools, however, we find spirits of place in locations like swimming pools, locker rooms, and libraries. Dormitories function like hotels, with many changes and lots of psychic disturbance in a small place. For those spirits that are particularly interested in the experiences of childhood and which take an interest in consuming those experiences, a school can become a permanent home; but it's just as common for a spirit to move on once the children they are interested in grow up and move on themselves.

Libraries

For similar reasons as universities and schools, libraries can also be subjects of haunting. These hauntings can again come due to affection to particular topics or ideas, and libraries are home to their own family of spirits of place, spirits of learning and education and study. Wherever knowledge is held, spirits can be found, and so libraries are opportune for spirits of place. It is uncommon to find malevolent spirits in libraries. In situations where the library has gained notoriety for being "haunted," it is generally because spirits have found they can gain worship in the form of ghost hunts and attention through the manifestation of apparitions or poltergeist phenomena, or through otherwise making themselves known. This kind of attention seeking behavior is not a threat or danger. Instead, it is merely an attempt at gaining the power that comes from being an object of worship and offering. Such a spirit benefits when a library gains a reputation for being haunted, as this can encourage visitors and so increase door counts and patron numbers. Much more commonly, libraries do not consider themselves haunted places. Nevertheless, students who make offerings or acknowledge the local spirits in their visits to the library are likely to benefit.

Prisons

Prisons also often attract rumors of hauntings; though until they are closed it is generally not possible to investigate these claims. The atmosphere of a prison is neither friendly nor happy, and unlike hospitals, which at least come with the promise of treatment and recovery, in most cases prisons, at least in the United States, are strictly punitive rather than rehabilitative. This literally oppressive atmosphere creates an impression of misery that is only amplified in the absence of inmates as the building becomes abandoned and dilapidated. Of the larger abandoned prisons with frequent claims of hauntings that I have visited[6], the types of spirits typically present are those that feed on misery or take pleasure in the kinds of criminal activities that have occurred there, as well as religious spirits that minister to the incarcerated. I've found that cases of hauntings as such are difficult to nail down. Prisons are

---

[6] Alcatraz is probably the most famous closed prison in the US, and naturally has stories of hauntings. Less known but popular in ghost hunting circles is the West Virginia Penitentiary in Moundsville, WV.

large places, and the hauntings of such places tend to be specific to cells or blocks or areas, and not to the entire prison. Divination rituals may be necessary to even find the spirits we're looking for. Abandoned prisons, unlike many other abandoned sites, don't tend to be left unguarded and can be difficult to get access to. As for active prisons, if anyone is so unfortunate as to find themselves incarcerated and should want to practice the techniques in this book, the results would be interesting at least.

Groves, Woods, and Forests

Groves, woods, forests, and so on are the home to a wide variety of nature spirits and frequently the subject of animistic traditions which recognize that all things have spirits. When "haunted," these places typically take on foreboding appearances and impressions. Overgrowth may be much thicker, and light blocked by trees or other obstructions. An eerie sense of calm and quiet can come, and we often find fog even at times of day when we would not expect it. Fog, like smoke, is easy for spirits to manipulate, and hauntings of groves or woods is often accompanied by fog that behaves in strange ways.

The spirits of groves, woods, and forests are usually interested in the protection and cultivation of their land. Such places with a reputation for being haunted have often gained it through years of thinking of that land as holy or sacred. In North America, this often predates European colonization, and as many of the North American indigenous religions were animistic, these spirits are used to a kind of veneration and respect that they no longer receive. Because of this, the more powerful nature guardians often protect their favored lands aggressively, attempting to elicit responses from people. Those who show veneration and respect are left alone, while those who hold disagreeable opinions or beliefs, or who do things which are obnoxious to the spirits are harassed or haunted.

Paradoxically, this can cause people who believe in nature spirits not to encounter them, while those who do not believe ignore their encounters or dismiss them as simply being "spooky" and carry on with their business.

Local folk tradition is often the best indicator of what kinds of behaviors or beliefs these spirits prefer people to hold. In the absence of human caretakers of forests and groves, magical practitioners or pagans who have developed relationships with the spirits already are good sources of information about the local spirits. If we cannot find or contact these human protectors of nature (often they find us, if we begin a working somewhere), we can look to the beliefs and ideas of local and indigenous peoples. We should take into account that while the mechanics of a belief may be preserved accurately, the explanatory stories of a folk tradition will change over time to stay relevant. So, woodland spirits who prioritize growth but accept the natural cycle of destruction and creation may be understood, but the stories of how those spirits have come to be may change from generation to generation in the local population. In cases where such ideas are lost, they may be misunderstood as haunting spirits, or potential paranormal encounters like the "Mothman," "Goatman," or "Bigfoot." In these cases, the kinds of experiences people have are maintained (fear and dread, for example, or seeing a monster) but the reasoning behind it has been lost. Folklore sometimes preserves the direct experiences of people without the tradition that would explain *why* they have those experiences.

Veneration and respect for the forest as well as the spirit (and indeed these two cannot really be separated) is the primary goal and need of such spirits. Making a small offering or even simply acknowledging its presence is usually sufficient to pacify such hauntings, but in no case can the spirit be "driven off" or appeased *universally*. Even if one achieves a personal knowledge and friendship of the great oaken spirits that protect a forest, when the loggers come that spirit will not be happy nor friendly, and generally will not discriminate in that upset between the loggers themselves and other people, no matter how long those other people have lived there. After all, is it not the responsibility of those other people to protect such a spirit and tree from other humans? Similarly, hunters often have a relationship with the land on which they hunt, and hunters more familiar to the land will often have more success, especially if their attitude is respectful and especially if they are hunting for food or subsistence rather than purely for sport. Meanwhile, commercial hunting operations without respect for nature or life will not often find the support of the land on which they occur. While that doesn't necessarily mean the hunt will be unsuccessful – a bullet kills a deer regardless – there won't be as many obstacles in the case of the former.

Nature spirits are generally fairly hierarchical, with local spirits being numerous but not very powerful, under the protection of greater spirits of areas, themselves being projected aspects of even greater spirits of regions, and so on. In this case, cultivation of relationships with the higher spirits that are more vast and influential can be beneficial, but often bridges the gap into the religious experience.

While I acknowledge the existence of gods and demigods, it isn't pertinent to the subject to discuss the cultivation of religious worship or practice of nature magic. For those interested, they should refer to books more specific to the practice of nature worship or pagan reconstruction. Hauntings in woods or natural features tend to be expressed through the actions of much more local spirits. Large, region ruling spirits may manifest in weather events or make themselves known through cataclysms or interference with human affairs, but manifesting to frighten off some random humans is well beneath them. This tends to be the work of much more local spirits operating on a much smaller level.

The animistic spirits are not the only ones that can be found in woods, and in the Celtic traditions as well as those of Northern European woodlands can also be the haunts of faeries and other similar beings which are essentially human-like in their nature and characteristics. These spirits may not be humanoid. They exist in an incorporeal way, but their birth is that of a similar karma to human beings, and they have similar intelligences, likes, dislikes, personalities, and so on. They are what Buddhists would consider in the "human realm" despite not being human beings. As they do not have physical bodies, they can only manipulate our world indirectly, often powerfully, through magic, just as we interact with their world through magic. Sometimes, this magic can be dramatic and obvious, other times it is less so. In any case, it is important to approach these spirits as cautiously and politely as we would unfamiliar human beings, and not to treat them as simply another species of animal with predictable behaviors. In fact, we will rarely encounter intelligent spirits that are so easily predictable.

In many locations, the woodland spirits will be named and their general properties known and reflected in the folklore of the region. For example, West Virginia has the Mothman, Central Maryland has the Snallygaster, and New Jersey has the Jersey Devil. While these are described as living beings, monsters, or beasts, we can often trace their origins to spirits. The Snallygaster, for example, comes from the German term "schneller Geist," or "quick ghost." Over time the legend has changed such that it is now more of a dragon that swoops from the skies. But dragons are another example of a spiritual force sometimes described as physical. The Jersey Devil is itself often associated with the Pine Barrens Witch and so believed to be a spirit as well. And while the Mothman is a more recent phenomenon, it bears consideration that it may be a new explanation for an old phenomenon.

Lakes, Ponds, Rivers, and Streams

Like the nature spirits of forests and woodlands, lakes, ponds, and bodies of water are also inhabited by their own spirits. In the Tibetan tradition these are called *lu*, in India *nagas*. In North America, they are often called simply *water spirits*. These spirits are intrinsically associated with water and so it is generally important to keep them happy as they can bring rain or drought. Because they live in water, offerings to them are usually deposited into a body of water. Spills of hazardous or noxious materials, drought that dries up streams and ponds, or wanton disrespect for bodies of water will often cause these spirits vexation. Like faeries, nagas are in the human realm, and while some can be understanding and patient, others will be quick to anger and fast to action. Dealing with nagas is often a delicate affair. It is important not to anger them, because their powers often include control over rains. Droughts and dry spells can result from upset nagas, and propitiating them can help ensure a healthy growing season.

Because water is an element particularly associated with psychic phenomena and greatly affected by the lunar phases, there are astrological considerations for what days are acceptable for contacting or making offerings to nagas. Because contacting them on the wrong days is often worse than not contacting them at all, this class of spirit is perhaps best left alone, and working with them will not be a goal of this book. It is important to know, however, that this same lunar and water elemental affinity makes nagas particularly able to affect the human realm, and so it is unwise to anger them. Like humans, the patience of individuals varies, and they can be incited merely by trying to contact them incorrectly or by offering incorrect incense. It is generally best to leave nagas on their own and simply respect bodies of water without dealing too much with these beings unless one has been properly trained.

Bodies of water can also be the home to *undines*, a type of *elemental spirit*. These are spirits who embody the characteristics of their element, essentially a kind of spiritual living intelligence of the element's presence in a place or process. Elemental spirits can inhabit or abide in anything of their own element, and so fire elementals (called *salamanders*) can be found in fire. *Gnomes*, as already discussed can be found in earth, homes or underground. *Sylphs* can be found high in the sky in clouds, on the top of high mountains, an on the sides of cliffs. Undines and other elemental spirits are usually interested only in the processes of their elemental nature. They may be interested in protecting a body of water, but more likely are interested in the flowing or seeping of the water. In any case, they are much more commonly encountered when called to rather than making contact on their own. When they do make contact on their own, it is usually through the vehicle of their element. Like nagas and other water spirits, elemental spirits will make themselves known by causing floods or rains or droughts. It is uncommon for them to appear as apparitions, but when they do folkloric accounts present them as not unlike mermaids.

Historical Sites, Battlefields and Sites of Trauma

Many of the above locations are amplified in their effect or activity due to being some kind of historically significant site, and I would be neglectful not to discuss these sites separately and as a group. It is a long-held contention in the paranormal investigation community that these more historically important sites tend to be more haunted, a perception perhaps reinforced by the fact that it is only the fantastic, ominous, or interesting haunted sites that make the cut on television shows and books about hauntings and paranormal phenomena. This comes down merely to an issue of ratings. Any paranormal investigator with any real experience on the job will testify that while the historically interesting sites may be more dramatic or impressive, while those investigations have more *gravitas*, these sites tend to be no more haunted than 13 Anystreet Drive,

Anytown, USA. It is their prominence in our minds that tends to make these historical site hauntings seem much more significant. The stories we associate with the events of the haunting lend power to those phenomena. The interest and veneration from around the world strengthens the site no differently than a church or place of worship. After all, every location is a place where history has occurred, what we remember is only the history that has affected great numbers of people. For the people involved at the time, the history of any unknown house may have been far more important than any number of battles.

Battlefields

Battlefields can be particularly haunted locations due to the existence of beings that feed on that energy particularly. Crows are a symbol of battle because of their appearance after the fighting has ended, picking over the remains of the deceased. Just as crows descend upon the fresh battleground, so do various spirits of war, disharmony, and discord flock to such sites and remain to feast on the residual energy. When we memorialize these locations as monuments to battle, making them into national parks and tourist attractions, these spirits can find themselves a permanent home. What is a battlefield park but a monument to war? For spirits of war and discord, this is a temple.

Many people report seeing apparitions of the battle played out by spectral soldiers many years after the battle has concluded. Here the case of the psychic impressions left on the land becomes much more likely. These battlefields are powerful places, and the impression of them is carried through time by their memorialization. Because we set aside the battlefield as a monument to the battle, that energy of war persists. In the dark of night, sensitive to suggestion and projection under the moon, it is easy for the thoughts of not just the soldiers whose traumatic deaths left lasting psychic impressions to manifest, but for all that we know of the battle to play itself out before us. Spirits, too, come to these places and can participate in such spectral projections. It's common for the psychic impression to play a major part in the *particulars* of the apparition. Spirits of war and discord may show us many things; but when they haunt a particular battleground, why not show us that battle, so easily accessible in the energy of a place?

Sites of Trauma

Similarly, sites of murders, torture, or traumatic events create impressions like this. The mind is brought into sharp, singular focus during traumatic and unexpected events, and this can leave an impression on the energy of a place. In addition, the knowledge of the people visiting the haunt feeds into this lasting impression. Later visitors' awareness of the events may be all that is necessary to bring that familiar sense of unease. Knowing that people died in a room, that horrible crimes took place in a room, but with no evidence of this before us, is unsettling. It reminds us of our own mortality and the fragility of our own comfort. If any living room can appear as the haunted one does now, while at the same time be subject to transformation into a horrific crime scene spattered in blood and brain, then how can we remain comfortable in the familiarity of a place? And so this uneasy contradiction puts us in a state particularly susceptible to influence of the paranormal, or the projection from our own mind of the same.

Many investigations of these places speculate that some demon or evil spirit not only inhabits the place at the time of the investigation or haunting, but that this same demon or evil spirit must have been the *cause* of the murder or crime or so on. While this is possible, I am not keen on this particular interpretation. I do think that such events can be the cause or condition of the *birth* of such a spirit or demon. A person who commits such a crime creates the karma of being reborn as a demon or evil spirit, whose misery lives forward, and the significance of the location and the karmic ties to the place can lead to such a demon being born in that place. I think then that it is likely that the particularly miserable, suffering, malevolent spirit, the demon, comes *after* the horrific act, as a *result* of the horrific act, and not as commonly as a cause of the same. Similarly, the occurrence of such a crime at a location can increase the circumstances or conditions that might lead to an evil spirit being born in that place; but again, in this case the traumatic event occurs *first*. Certainly I cannot deny that at times the possession or influence of powerful and evil spirits can cause these kinds of behaviors in people, and we will discuss this in a later chapter, but I am reluctant to jump to this conclusion *initially*. If there is evidence of the haunting before the tragedy happened, then of course this should be considered; otherwise, we should look at the facts as they are in time. If there is some motivation for an evil spirit to do this, some kind of personal benefit, then of course we should consider that.

Ultimately, though, it does not really matter. Whether the spirit caused or resulted from a historical event makes no difference to us now if the spirit is there *now*, haunting a place *now*. Overall, though, it is very rare that a spirit will directly compel another person to do such a thing. Perhaps, though, the mere presence of a spirit can *encourage* that kind of thinking, through exposing us to the energy and thought of the intention to do violence. So, it becomes very difficult to discern at which point a haunting has occurred in places where murders or crimes are committed routinely or where history repeats itself again and again. It is easy to imagine that, after moving into a house known to be haunted and known to be the site of a murder, our minds may return again and again to the thought of murder such that when the impetus arises, we simply act according to how our minds have habituated themselves. In a sense, the spirit may have caused this, but not in the sense of through possession, compulsion, or mind control. Ultimately it is difficult to draw a line between a spirit-caused event and a spirit resulting from an event.

I would also caution a different approach in befriending demons which are purely manifested of anger and hatred. For these it is important to remember that this anger and hatred is a form of suffering. We can take a piteous attitude of compassion towards them, but I would not encourage one to become too familiar. We can show compassion, and make offerings in hope that they will become pacified and find happiness, and we should. But associating too closely runs the risk of the same spirit influencing us to act out their malevolent agenda. So, we must be kind but cautious. It is perhaps best to simply offer to the spirit to leave you alone and consider changing its ways, and not to ask for favors or information. Better instead to kindly send the spirit on its way. While some spirits do require more forceful measures to subdue, my approach is always first to extend an offer in generosity and kindness, as nobody likes to suffer, and nobody likes to be fearful, not even "evil" or malicious spirits.

Ley Lines and Nexuses

It would again be neglectful for me not to discuss ley lines, as these are often mentioned in the energetic and magical community and can serve as another condition which makes a place more likely to be haunted. Ley lines are natural lines of subtle energy or power that connect between "nodes" of energetic power, astrological landmarks, and so on. In the 1920s, amateur archaeologist Alfred Watkins noticed that major sites of historical importance were intersected by geometric lines. Of course, any two points can have a line drawn between them, so it is not sufficient to determine ley lines simply by sitting with a map and drawing lines between points. Watkins proposed that ancient peoples may have traced these lines out, resulting in geographical anomalies that mark important points and correspond with celestial landmarks. While the existence of ley lines remains contested by even the mainstream archaeological community, their existence has been widely embraced by the occult and esoteric communities.

Today there are not always obvious and evident physical markers denoting ley lines. Geomancy and astrology can help locate these spots, but so can simple observation and divination such as by pendulum or map dowsing. Wherever ancient monuments are found, they can generally be assumed to be located along ley lines. Even if these were not naturally occurring ley lines it is likely that the presence of the monument, temple, or shrine, if significant, will have created one. Any place where major religious observances or especially major conjurations occurred historically may very well be along a ley line. When people perform conjurations, evocations, or the like, doing so along ley lines can draw from the local energy and make the magic work that much more effective.

Spirits also recognize these places of power. Ley lines are a large aspect of the world's energetic cartography, and spirits are more likely to come to these places. They also are able to appear with more dramatic effects when in these places, as the charged energy gives spirits more to "work with" when manipulating the physical plane or the minds of people on it. Just as the conjurer will draw on the energy from a ley line to improve the strength of her evocation, spirits can draw on that power when they magically interact with our world. If apparitions, poltergeists, or other manifestations in an area are particularly strong, the presence of a ley line or node should not be ruled out.

There is some question as to whether ley lines exist prior to, or as a result of, places of power such as cemeteries, churches, and so on. Because these sorts of ancient sites exist along alleged ley lines, it can be difficult to tell. We know that ancients chose to build their monuments in locations for reasons, but we do not know if the presence of ley lines factored into those reasons. After all, a Stonehenge monument is built in alignments with celestial bodies, but whether the presence of ley lines factored into its placement is anyone's guess.

I am personally inclined to believe that we create these ley lines through the arrangement of our significant monuments, and that they do not exist prior to the significance of the site. That does little to change the power that comes from a ley line crossing even an insignificant site. It's not unheard of to check a map for significant locations (cemeteries and so like) only to find that a haunting we are investigating is directly between two such locations. But it is the significance we've ascribed that creates this effect. Watkins himself never proposed a spiritual significance to ley lines, instead considering them common-sense arrangements of roads between significant sites.

For most of our purposes, ley lines are disruptive rather than productive. While it can be helpful for a spirit to have a stronger influence, these lines are usually accompanied with a significant amount of psychic noise. Whether this is a result of some kind of natural flow of energy from consciousness or a property of the earth itself is irrelevant; the energetic throughput makes it more difficult to attend to the subtle energies of spirits. A spirit trying to communicate with small energetic nudges will be drowned out in the flow. Many of the sites we discuss here have some kind of energetic significance, but few are significant because of the energy itself. It is somewhat exclusive to ley lines that the movement of energy is itself the reason for the significance.

Crossroads and Crypts

Earlier we discussed beings that are attracted to liminality and transitional states. These are some of the spirits most attracted to crossroads, cemeteries, and other places traditionally understood to be haunted. Where cemeteries are often believed to be haunted by the spirits of the dead and those with an interest in them, crossroads hold a place in folk lore, myth, and magic as representative of the unknown, liminality, and change. Both cemeteries and crossroads exist as a kind of spiritual "international waters." Cemeteries represent the final rite of passage through which all human beings pass, and in mythology and folklore house not only restless spirits of the deceased—which I actually find uncommon[7]—but also protectors, psychopomps, and religious figures that watch over the cemetery as sacred ground. Crossroads, because of their symbolic nature as representing the unknown and the in between, are associated with meeting the devil or spirits to make a bargain. They are the traditional home of deities like Hekate, Trivia, Papa Legba, and their associated servants.

Cemeteries

Cemeteries are the traditional haunts not only of spirits, but of sorcerers and magicians interested in mysticism and necromancy. The defining feature of the mystic is the abnegation of the ego, the rejection of the self and the renunciation of secular life. In Christian mysticism, this involves for example the Rosicrucian concept of returning to oneness with God. In Islam, Sufism encourages a similar result.

---

[7] According to the Tibetan Buddhist tradition, after death our consciousness is untethered from the deceased physical body and spends up to forty days roaming about based on our habitual tendencies. Some people will fixate on their body, and follow it to the cemetery, but most do not stay long. After a time, the spirit will instead travel about visiting loved ones, favorite places, and so on. This spirit travels instantly, directed by thought, as our consciousness does when untethered from the body.

In Buddhism, one rejects the concept of self entirely and seeks to attain enlightenment. In all of these cases, a focus on one's own mortality is central. If this self is impermanent, if we will certainly die, then what point in focusing merely on our own worldly benefit or improvement? Because sorcery and mysticism often go hand in hand—and I would argue that generally the latter is necessary to advance past a certain point in the former—sorcery itself is often associated with this focus on death. Some associate the skull with evil, but when used as a symbol by mystics and sorcerers it has no evil associations at all. Instead, it serves as a reminder of one's own fragility and certain death.

However, because of this association with evil and witchcraft, the cemetery's reputation as a haunted place often takes on a dark tone. Considerably darker rituals such as zombification in voodoo and other magical traditions have contributed to this. Ultimately, however, the greatest cause of fear in graveyards is the symbolic reminder of our own inevitable demise. Couple this with a media that reinforces that the cemetery is a dark and frightening place, and it is easy to understand why it grabs our attention as a potentially haunted spot. It is frightening *without* the presence of spirits, all the while rarely being free of them.

Most commonly, cemeteries are inhabited by protective spirits and land guardians, especially in countries where there are strong familial guardian spirits. Ancestor worship itself sustains these familial protector spirits, and those protectors often stay to prevent the remains of family members from being desecrated or disturbed. These same guardian spirits also receive sustenance from offerings left at the grave site, such as food or flowers, and can be strengthened by these. Other spirits may also begin accepting these offerings and over time grow to become part of the family's spiritual retinue.

Other spirits commonly found haunting cemeteries are death and decay-eating spirits that sustain themselves on consuming the spiritual essence of decay. These spirits take up permanent residence in cemeteries because they know they can find a sure meal, but they are unlikely to be found at significantly older or disused family cemeteries as the remains there will have long since finished decaying. One of the more prominent haunted houses I've visited was a small Civil War era house in Maryland with a small graveyard on the property, the protectors of which were upset that it was being neglected and were eager to discuss the matter with me as I was the first sensitive person to have come along in some time. As a child, I didn't realize what was really going on, just that there were spirits haunting me and they wanted something I could not provide. When I visited the house again years later, the graveyard had been cared for much more, and the apparitions and manifestations that had occurred before did not recur.

This is an example of a lot of conditions coming together for a haunting event to occur. A sensitive individual who is psychically active coming to the house provided an audience for the local protectors, who had not been contacted in some time, to make some things known. Though I attended to them, I couldn't give them what they needed, so eventually they left me alone for the night. All told, it was not nearly the most eventful contact I've had with spirits or cemetery ghosts, but it left an impression on me at the time, having been one of the clearest early contacts I had with cemetery spirits.

Because of their status as frightening places in our minds, cemeteries are also a prime location for legend tripping, where adolescents seek to prove their bravery by undertaking challenges or overcoming obstacles laid out in local legends. Because this can sometimes result in the teenagers performing acts of magical ritual, it becomes very difficult to determine the actual presence of other occult activity. While one might disregard the rituals performed by teenagers during a legend-trip as ineffectual games or stories, this neglects that essentially *any* action can become magically significant if it is performed with intent and concentration of will towards bringing about an effect. The evil eye, for example, need not be performed by a witch or sorcerer; anyone who focuses their ill intent on someone else can be said to be casting the evil eye. Rituals performed in graveyards to bring about spirit contacts need not be elaborate or well-designed rituals of ancient ceremonial provenance; simply the intentionality and belief of the legend trippers may well be sufficient to have an effect, especially if the ritual has been well established and repeated through local lore.

We must also consider that graveyards and cemeteries are magically active and charged on their own. Any ritual performed in a cemetery is more likely to pack some punch than the same ritual performed in, say, a living room. I am skeptical of the idea that the locations of most cemeteries, at least modern ones, were selected based on any other criteria than the ease of performing burials and the value of the land. It seems that cemeteries, by virtue of their symbolism as a liminal threshold, or because of the strong ideas people associate with them, become energetically active over time. Certainly modern cemeteries are chosen due to convenience and market pressures more than for their power, so we can conclude that cemeteries are powerful in their own right.

Crossroads

Crossroads are not necessarily known for being *haunted*, but because of their place in folklore and legend as places to meet with spirits, they deserve some mention. Admittedly, crossroads are more important within this book for their significance in magic, as a place to meet spirits or to drive them off. In the latter case, bringing spirits to a crossroads is believed to be able to confuse them and make them less likely to return to a house. During Tibetan New Year celebrations, spirits that cause obstacles to the household are driven out and chased to nearby crossroads. The hope is that they will be unable to find their way back. This is just one example of crossroads not as a place to meet spirits but to dispense with them. For the most part, however, in the West we tend to consider crossroads a place to meet spirits.

The association of crossroads with the occult, with mysteries and the unknown, dates back at least as far Ancient Greece and Rome. The Roman goddess *Trivia*, meaning "three ways," rules over witchcraft, the occult, graveyards, and, of course, crossroads. In Greece, this same role was filled by Hekate, who even today enjoys a healthy mystery cult as a patroness and tutelary deity of sorcerers and occultists of all sorts. In the Haitian Vodou tradition, a fair few Loa are said to be meetable at crossroads, not the least of which is Papa Legba. In folklore and legend, crossroads are considered a good place to meet the devil to make an infernal pact in return for worldly power. It is a sort of running gag among musicians that meeting the devil at a crossroads and trading one's soul is a way to gain supernatural skill. While I can't personally vouch for making infernal pacts at crossroads, I do think that they are valuable locations to perform workings and to contact spirits, deities, and their representatives. If looking to find spirits with which to forge relations, a crossroads would be a good place to start. Offerings and rituals at crossroads can be used to bring spirits, and this same methodology can be used to remove spirits from locations, by making offerings at the crossroads to those *specific* spirits with a request that they not return.

Crossroads, perhaps even more so than cemeteries, represent liminality and interstitial states, and so they serve as valuable conduits to contact the spirit realm. It is considered good form to use crossroads ritually in summonings and banishings both, but generally it would be considered poor form to do so wrathfully. Crossroads represent meeting places and happenstance, and the use of forceful means when conjuring at a crossroads is the spiritual equivalent of a highwayman strong-arming travelers. In the chapter on conjuration we will discuss some rituals for conjuration as well as dismissing spirits using crossroads, as well as how to practically apply the concept of liminality to ritual workings. Within buildings there are also crossroads, in the liminal thresholds of doors and hallways, and these areas can be exploited to interact with spirits. By leaving offerings or performing rituals in the between spaces of buildings, we can reach into the between spaces of reality and hope to pull out those spirits that walk between worlds.

Thresholds

All of these spaces – crossroads, doorways, entry-halls, cemeteries, and so on – represent a state of being in-between. This is what is meant by a "liminal space." A doorway is a space neither in nor out. An entry-hall is a space where we've left one place and are going into another but have not yet arrived there. Crossroads are places in our journey where we must make a decision, and until we do so we remain in an undetermined state between steps in a journey. As mentioned, cemeteries demonstrate the transition between life and death, the final liminal threshold of all sentient beings. These critical stages of being in-between represent raw creative potential as well as the uncertainty of having left a comfortable place for the relative unknown of the future. For this reason, spirits that haunt these kinds of places are often able to help us in making decisions or creating turning points in our lives.

The sorcerer lives taking each moment as a potential liminal state, working in the in-between spaces: between moments, between situations, between worlds. Spirits of crossroads and crypts, therefore, can be powerful allies or troublesome enemies, but they are rarely malicious. Instead, they give us choices, and like the choice of the crossroad determines where we will find ourselves in the road, the choice at the spiritual crossroad can determine the direction our life takes. These spirits are powerful, but they are not harmful. They simply give us options that we must choose between.

Possessions and Personal Hauntings

While hauntings are typically associated with places, a *possession* or personal haunting takes place when a spirit takes an interest in a specific person. Broadly speaking, the reasons for these are similar to why spirits haunt locations: something about the person is attractive to the spirit, either because the spirit likes those qualities or because of some other connection to the person, such as the person offering the spirit something they cannot get elsewhere. Because people are diverse, however, there are many more things that may attract a spirit. People can have any number of qualities which can attract spirits, from family upbringing to life decisions to inclinations and habits to experiences. Additionally, the interconnected karmic network of past lives can attract spirits to us. Connections we've made in previous lives through our activities, beliefs, family, and so on can leave spirits indebted or otherwise connected to us. Protectors of families, known through various cultures as guardian angels, family geniuses, or protector spirits, are usually attached to the members of that family regardless even of if the family still believes in those spirits.

Forceful Possession

In possession, spirits seize control over a person's body, or exercise a strong influence over his or her mind. This can last for a brief moment or a very long time. It is often an unpleasant and generally non-consensual experience; and it is disturbing not only for the victim but for those around him or her. Cases of possession are relatively rare and usually brief, most typically occurring in children. The spirit may either trap the mind of the victim in a hallucination while controlling the body's behavior in his or her absence, or seize control of the body forcefully, moving the body about puppet-like while the conscious mind of the victim watches helpless. In the former case, the victim usually has no recollection or memory of what happened, as in a dissociative fugue. In the latter case, on the other hand, they may vividly remember all of it. This can contribute significantly to post-traumatic stress.

It goes without saying that the spirits involved here are not generally friendly or kind. We must understand in these cases that the best resolutions do not come from hasty assumptions about the nature of the spirits involved. All too often people will immediately go to the exorcists of their own religious tradition, or seek out Catholic exorcists due to the popularity of the rite of exorcism. These rites often make assumptions about the spirit that make it more difficult to deal with the situation before it gets better. Usually, the best information about a possession can be gained by simply engaging in a dialogue, no matter how disturbing this may be. Even if direct answers are not received, enough clues can be gathered from observation to determine the nature of the spirit involved and refer to the correct spiritual tradition. Exorcism in the Christian or Wiccan or Buddhist traditions may work well with spirits of those traditions, but what works best is the exorcism from a tradition that recognizes the relevant spirit. Performing exorcisms on spirits that do not recognize the spiritual authority of the exorcist is unlikely to be fruitful, or will be much more tedious as the exorcist must first establish the spiritual authority. If we instead use the methods of exorcism pertinent to that particular spirit, authority can be asserted that the spirit will immediately recognize.

These days, spirits are not bound regionally or culturally such that the local tradition is the most relevant. We must investigate and discover the spirit's nature and its own cultural background before simply jumping in. Such information can also give us clues as to what the spirit may want. Possession seems to take a lot of energy, either in the deception of a person or the physical overpowering of their mind's control over the body. Because of this, it is usually safe to assume that the spirit is not doing the possession merely for fun or entertainment. It can't be ruled out that the spirit isn't demonstrating its power or engaging in some arrogant display, but more often than not there is something else going on.

Supernatural possession, where a spirit takes control directly of a living creature's form, is a universally and cross-culturally recognized phenomenon. While the exact understandings of the mechanisms differ, the event is recognized in some form in cultures throughout the world. Typically contrasted with specifically demonic possession in the West, supernatural possession, or possession by spirits (rather than specifically by demons, a particular belief) is not always a malevolent thing.

When it is, however, we should not conjure or work with these spirits triflingly, with few exceptions. Doing so can give the spirit a bridge or create a karmic connection allowing the spirit to attack the investigator or ritualist. After all, if a spirit is capable of possessing a human, willingly or unwillingly, and we invite it into our presence, we're absolutely playing with fire. Instead, it is better to encourage them to move on. The more advanced sorcerer may take an interest in this kind of practice, but I would suggest it is best to avoid interacting with possessing spirits beyond what must be done to end the possession. Our obligation in this case is to the possessed person, and ensuring his or her safety; but we cannot do this at the cost of our own safety.

Oracles

In some cases, friendly spirits use the method of possession for useful or beneficial communication. For example, in Tibet, oracles perform elaborate rituals to become possessed by patron spirits who temporarily control their body in order to deliver messages or prophecy. The Nechung Oracle, the State Oracle of Tibet, is perhaps the most famous of these, an oracle who invokes and is possessed by a spirit known as Dorje Drakden. This spirit is a *gyalpo*, or king spirit, and an oathbound protector of His Holiness the Dalai Lama. When the Nechung Oracle, having performed an elaborate invocation ritual, becomes possessed by Dorje Drakden, he is able to give information based on the spirit's knowledge and make predictions and prophecies to the His Holiness Dalai Lama about future or current events. During the ritual, the Oracle temporarily loses control of his body, becoming inhumanly strong. He dances and struts about unnaturally while speaking in an ancient dialect of Tibetan rarely understood by bystanders.

In this case, the possessing spirit is beneficial, and while the display of unnatural movement can be disconcerting to those not prepared for it, for people familiar with the process, it is not at all disturbing. As an invocation, this is expected. It is only when a possession is uninvited or unwelcome that we consider it a possession.

In other cases, spirits take control of animals in order to appear to people. It may be easier for a spirit to seize control of an animal than to manifest itself in a material form. Ultimately, it can be quite difficult to differentiate these. Except in obvious cases where the possessed animal is known to a person, there is not always strong evidence that the manifested person or creature is in fact physically present at all. After all, it could be an illusory display appearing as a real thing to us for the purpose of communication. Within Buddhism, for example, Buddhas or bodhisattvas often manifest as animals or people in unrecognizable forms to impart information or lessons or help. These people or animals are indistinguishable from "normal" people or animals arising from the play of cause and effect. Within Christendom, particularly within the charismatic movement, possession by the Holy Ghost leaves people speaking in tongues or demonstrating "holy laughter." This is of course contrasted with "demonic possession," though in both cases the person temporarily loses control of their own body under the influence of a spirit external to their own.

We cannot assume that all possessions are necessarily unfriendly, and so we should look instead at how they manifest. When the behaviors associated with the possession are harmful or injurious, we of course must treat this as unfriendly, regardless of the motivation of the spirit. Similarly, when a possession is involuntary and the spirit knows this, we can't really consider it friendly. When the possession is not causing a person to come into harm, then it is more reasonable to negotiate. In any case, it is important to maintain boundaries. When a medium invites a spirit to take control of his or her body it is perfectly fine. It is when the spirit is acting against our own will that we must draw firm lines of behavior. Because the victims of possession are often children, it is important to also ensure that other children are kept away from the possessing spirit when possible, or also taught how to draw firm boundaries. Protective magic may be necessary in some cases, and this will be discussed as well in the second part of the book.

Personal Haunting

Personal hauntings can be categorized by the connection between the person and the spirit. In some cases, a spirit has become attracted to a person for some reason or has a prior connection of some sort. In others, a spirit may be sent after a person, as in a curse. While the latter is somewhat uncommon, the malicious actions of others may lead to either the same sorts of experiences one might have from a haunting, or even to spirits being sent to haunt a person directly. In the case where spirits are being set against a person, it is not also likely that they will be able to be bought off or propitiated to leave; at least not cheaply. The sorcerer sending them, after all, will have already cultivated a relationship. But, it may be that these spirits will have been coerced or forced into the behavior and can be stopped through propitiation, so as always I advocate this as the first action. If an unfriendly haunting spirit cannot be won over by propitiation and offering, then one should begin to consider the possibility that the haunting is the result of a cursing, and appropriate measures should be taken. Properly protecting yourself from a curse where someone has sent spirits against you to cause harm is well outside the scope of this book, but as usual, knowing the tradition from which a curse is coming can be helpful. Communicating with the spirit and taking careful notes and making careful observations about everything that is going on, can yield clues which might reveal the origin and type of spirit or curse. Even if we cannot find more information ourselves, information can be provided to a professional sorcerer in consultation. Protecting yourself magically may or may not be effective depending on the spirits involved, and when dealing with magical defense I don't know that it's prudent for a beginner to take such things into his or her own hands alone.

Haunted Objects

Just as with places and persons, spirits can become fascinated by objects and take up residence with them. Objects can become *abodes*, or physical worldly homes in which the spirit lives and which serve as anchors for the spirit in the physical world. A sorcerer may create spirit houses as places to serve as homes for his or her retinue of spirits. Similarly, spirits can choose abodes for themselves. In other cases, haunted objects have no spirit involved and are not truly haunted. Instead, as in rooms where traumatic events have occurred, the object's subtle energy has been imprinted with some emotion, idea, memory, or so on. This is then felt by those around them. Because everyone has some faculty for interacting with subtle energy, everyone is able to sense this; but most people have no training or ability to discern the origin of their feelings. Unable to recognize psychometric reading, they assume that the object that makes them uncomfortable must be haunted.

Often, haunted objects gain a reputation through a pattern of actions. An object that is followed by tragedy and which brings misery to its owner is often called *cursed*. On the other hand, a good luck charm which brings fortune and benefit is called *blessed*. Both cursed and blessed objects can be powerful magical items created through ritual. Or they may be abodes of helpful spirits. The stereotypical genie in the bottle is an example of a magical device that holds a spirit ready to serve. While I've never encountered a bottle that could grant three wishes, as in stories, I have encountered objects with helpful spirits attached to them whose benefit belongs to whoever possesses the object. Amulets, charms, books, or really any somewhat durable object can house a spirit. Often, the object will relate to the spirit in some way. For example, a spirit of knowledge or wisdom may inhabit a book, while a spirit that attracts wealth may live in a gilded statue.

Statues and iconography of deities are also connected to the associated deity even if they are not homes for that deity per se. Representations are not the same as the thing itself, but they do create mental associations. Our actions towards statuary of spirits, towards Vodou *vedes,* towards Christian icons of saints, and so on all reveals our psychological intent towards the associated spirit. In some cases, powerful spirits may recognize this and choose to act. Because these statues can be similar to the spirit itself, it's wise to treat them as if the spirit were present even when it is not.

Haunted objects can be created either through intentional action or accidental impression. In certain forms of evocation, the spirit is forced into the object. For example, a spirit may be offered a number of different objects to serve as a home—called an abode—based on different classical elements. The chosen abode gives us some information about the spirit, including what kinds of divinations to use in the future when dealing with that spirit.

In some cases, however, there's no real way to tell. Objects, more than any other thing, tend to be something people infatuate with and attach to. People are likely to attach to their most prized and coveted possessions. When this attachment is exceptionally strong, people will be reborn as spirits that haunt the object. Of course, we must be careful when making this determination. When a person is particularly attached to an object, they will often leave a strong energetic impression of themselves on it. It is entirely possible that what may seem like a sentient spirit inhabiting a thing is actually just the impression of that person's personality left on the object over time. Usually a medium can make this determination fairly easily, however.

When haunted or cursed objects develop a strong reputation, it is not uncommon for them to become expensive artifacts. In some cases this will become their primary function. What may otherwise be a useless piece of junk can find new life when sold as a piece of paranormal paraphernalia. One should take caution when buying supposedly haunted goods, as this is an area rife for scams. In some cases, it is nothing more than fraud, with an unscrupulous person advertising something as haunted or cursed to sell it for more than it is worth. In other cases, a sorcerer may evoke a spirit into an object and sell it on. In this latter case the object is haunted as advertised, though the spirit may or may not be reliable for the stated purpose. An alleged protector spirit may not offer any protection at all to a purchaser of some amulet a sorcerer has stuffed them into and forgotten about. For the most part, if an object is being sold as having a spirit associated with it, I would assume it is fraud unless the source is of known reputation. Summoning your own spirits to inhabit objects is more likely to be beneficial anyhow.

Ghost Hunting and Paranormal Investigations

Ghost hunting and the active seeking of a paranormal experience has been an enduring pastime for generations, and remains a popular hobby today. Many enthusiasts and professionals prefer instead the more sterilized term "paranormal investigation." In the last few decades, the world of paranormal investigation has changed dramatically. New technologies allow for the recording of more specific measurements which paranormal investigators believe can indicate if not the presence of ghosts or spirits, at least the occurrence of a scientifically observable event. It seems in this way that like psychology's transition from a philosophical field about the nature of people's human experience into a medical field about the diagnosis of neurosis or psychosis and treatment using the biopsychosocial model, paranormal investigation has moved from the spiritualism of the late 19th and early 20th centuries to the attempt to scientifically quantify experiences in terms of electromagnetic fields, heat sensors, and various methods for allowing the recording of voices from beyond. I make no value judgement about this transformation, but note that in both cases the ultimate goal of the venture has changed. Why I distinguish ghost hunting and paranormal investigation is that the former term usually denotes much more casual efforts, without attempts to quantify objective experiences but rather the goal of merely having subjective experiences of the paranormal. The paranormal investigator instead focuses on collecting quantifiable data which supports or rejects the validity of a haunting event.

Both of these are important works. A recent move towards a kind of modern spiritualism using the tools and symbols of divination of our own generation – computers, cell phones, radio receivers, antennae, and the like – is a natural evolution of an innately human desire to contact other worlds and a universal fascination with the paranormal. Whereas in the past we used simpler techniques like talking boards to contact spirits, in today's technological era we can use electronic devices like the Ovilus or various EVP recorders to create interfaces through which ghosts may communicate. Like the field of *radionics*, which effects magic through a symbolic interface of wire, knobs, and switches, or the CyberWitch software which purportedly allows for the construction and casting of sigils on a screen intuitive for the Millennial generation, the embrace of modern technology by paranormal investigators is neither surprising nor out of place. It is only the unfortunate adoption of scientific materialism that hurts this movement.

If paranormal investigation becomes merely about using instruments to take measurements of a place, which is then used to confirm whether a haunting occurs, then at best we end up in the same place we already were when the haunting was suspected in the first place. Little is accomplished besides, perhaps, easing the uncertainty that experiencing paranormal phenomena can cause in the first place. When we focus only on metrics we lose sight of the real human experience of a haunting. We become blind to the *meaning* of a haunting, the *experience* of it. Instead of seeking contact with spirits, we seek cold spots or beeps on a machine. So while this pursuit is useful in validating experiences, it is useless in the actual mitigation, remediation, or exploration of the same. A heat sensor for example can only confirm the existence of changes in heat in a room, which cannot be demonstrated to be related to the paranormal. Electromagnetic sensors only demonstrate electromagnetic changes, but again, there is nothing linking this to a spirit. When we adopt the philosophy of scientific materialism along with its tools, it becomes impossible to make meaningful claims about the paranormal. After all, scientific materialism investigates the normal. If it could investigate the paranormal, the paranormal would just be normal. Because claims of haunting are so heavily related to actual human experiences, we can at best confirm that there are physical phenomena in the same places as experiential phenomena, but we cannot go further.

That's not to say we should reject these methods or their value. There is value in validating experiences in relation to physical phenomena as some people have a deep aversion to the idea that their experiences may not be true, or true as they understand them. Certainly, people may hallucinate because of unshielded wiring in old houses, or black mold, or other physical causes. Surely it is just as foolish to rule out mundane or secular causes of a haunting out of hand as it is to rule out spiritual causes. But the tools of paranormal investigation can be employed ritually or as part of a more complete, holistic approach to the spirits of an area. By combining the methods of physical measurement and spiritual investigation, we can create a much clearer picture of exactly what is going on, and in a way that is not only demonstrable, but also meaningful.

So what are the tools of paranormal investigation, and what are the characteristics of a ghost hunt differentiates it?

Many of the tools used by the modern ghost hunter or paranormal investigator are devices developed for the purpose of giving spirits methods for communication. Recorders are used to attempt to capture *electronic voice phenomena* (EVP) which are believed to be formed by spirits manipulating soundwaves. EVP is imperceptible to human ears, but it can be captured by the recorder and interpreted by a trained ear. White noise machines can also create a substrate which spirits can supposedly manipulate more easily than silence when shaping sounds to try to communicate. Another approach uses rapidly cycling radio station scanners that can be used to listen for meaningful sentences as it moves between stations. In terms of visible phenomena, the use of night-vision, infrared, and thermal imaging are common in trying to capture evidence of spirits, or images of the spirits themselves. Both audio and visual information like this mostly serves the purpose of confirming the presence of ghosts. Some, however, can also be used to give the spirits a means of communication.

Using randomized information to give spirits a method to communicate is not new. In the past, spiritualists would use talking boards or decks of cards or things like the motion of candles to focus attention. It is important to point out that many Spiritualist séances in the early 1900s were fraudulent, done for profit by recreating via sleight of hand the expected experiences of ghost hunters of the day, such as table tilting or the manifestation of "ectoplasm." The ease of fraud in these settings led in part to the decline of Spiritualism moving into the post-war era. It is difficult to dismiss all Spiritualist claims, however. Many legitimate mediums existed and exist within Spiritualist circles. Unfortunately, pressure to generate flashy, exciting results during séances led even legitimate mediums to deceive their clients some of the time. But, we would be a bit daft to deceive *ourselves* when attempting to contact spirits, so when performing séances ourselves this is less of a concern.

One common piece of equipment for paranormal investigation today are electromagnetic field detectors, which are used to detect changes in magnetic fields. When set up in stationary locations, they should not change often or inexplicably, so they are sometimes considered reliable in detecting the abnormal, if not necessarily the spiritual. Tools like the "Ovilus" series of paranormal research devices use this information to trigger words, phonemes, or so on from a dictionary based on the degree of environmental swings. How a spirit would know how to manipulate this box meaningfully I am unsure, but they are fairly popular amongst paranormal investigators today for their ability to deliver clear messages. For our purposes, they are useful for the potential to interpret or corroborate the information that comes through in part of a divination or conjuration.

While generally replaced with the more modern technology, random number generators have historically been used as interfaces for supernatural communication. For example, a binary random number generator producing "1" and "0" answers with regularity multiple times per second or so can be asked questions, with "1" for yes and "0" for no. Statistically significant frequencies of 1s and 0s are considered as potential "answers" when they occur within a timeframe of a question being asked. We can ask either the regular ghost hunting confirmatory questions,[8] or, as we will discuss later, we could ask other divinatory questions. In the case of divination, we're not interested in information about the spirit itself, but in information the spirit hopefully knows about something else.

Historically, ghost hunting has also served as a rite of passage, a kind of legend tripping, where teenagers or young adults make journeys to places of local legends and engage in behaviors to prove their bravery in relative safety. These feats of courage are formative and it is important for us all to challenge ourselves in our approach to the unknown. Lighting candles and chanting Bloody Mary, for example, serves as a challenge to the paranormal as well as a way of facing our fear in a situation where there is little real danger. The feeling of relief upon completion of the task is just as strong as when we perform physical feats of daring. Ghost hunting can be a form of legend tripping as well, and spirits can and do inhabit the places where legend trips occur. These trips serve as minor acts of worship or propitiation; attention given from a society that usually gives none. This kind of ghost hunt is usually less sophisticated technologically but ironically more often resembles the kind of activities we aim to perform in this book: actual contact and the cultivation of a relationship with a spirit.

---

[8] "Is there a spirit present?" "Do you mean harm?" "Are you unhappy with something?" and so on.

In legend trips this relationship is usually one of fear, but it is a relationship nonetheless.

In the late 1800s and early 1900s when spiritualism was at its height and the Theosophical movement was in full swing, ghost hunts and séances were a popular diversion. As mentioned before, séances and other attempts to contact spirits in late Spiritualism were often staged and fraudulent. Being a talented medium had become very profitable, and talent in this case meant the ability to reliably contact ghosts. I do not want to create the impression that talent means successful, reliable contact in this case. Contacting certain spirits often becomes very reliable as we build working relationships with the spirit realm, but contacting the specific haunting spirits we seek is not always workable, even if the techniques are performed correctly. It is the ability to perform these techniques accurately that indicates talent, more than the result. A talented hunter may not always find prey but always makes a good job of it, and so the talented medium or sorcerer may not always get results from a spell, but the spell should always be performed well. If one *never* or *rarely* has success, this may be cause for reevaluating one's approach, but a failure here or there should not be considered an indicator of inability. When working for others, the possibility for failure should always be communicated to clients beforehand.

Another classic staple of ghost hunts, again harkening back to the Victorian era, is that of the medium or psychic. This individual, through his or her own preternatural ability, is able to communicate with spirits either directly or through the use of divination techniques. While some such claims are fraudulent, most claims are legitimate and can be taken more or less at face value. Another type of paranormal personality, *inducers*, often cause haunting phenomena to occur with their mere presence. For whatever reason, inducers agitate spirits to action, be it in the form of manifestation or poltergeist activity. In some cases, inducers may just be psychokinetic individuals demonstrating RSPK when placed in "haunted" settings. Care must be taken when an inducer always seems to induce similar poltergeist activity and not other kinds of spiritual contact.

Beyond psychics or mediums, there are other methods of inducing paranormal activity in a place, which I also suggest we use during the initial stages of the investigation. Perhaps not *immediately,* but also not waiting until the time's up, we should consider the use of magic to improve our chances of finding the information we need. Most paranormal investigators are primarily focused on demonstrating whether or not something paranormal is happening, and nothing else. If that alone is our goal, then the use of magical methods of contacting spirits or getting them to appear and show their presence is not necessary. Obviously, doing so could poison the data; after all, there's no way to be certain that a spirit we summon through magic will be the spirit that was there before, and so even a positive finding of evidence of a haunting is useless if we intentionally caused a haunting as part of the investigation. The exact methods of contacting spirits or summoning them are discussed at great length in the later parts of this book, but I feel it necessary to mention them briefly here.

We don't have to go to great effort if we are investigating a haunting and the spirit is already manifesting, demonstrating PK, and so on. It's there, it's attending to us. Our attempts at communication can be very direct. Often, we simply need *think very loudly* and a spirit can reply. Other times speaking out loud is more effective (and serves the bonus of being easier to document so we know what a spirit was responding to). In these cases, we can usually skip directly to means of communicating with the spirit such as pendulum dowsing, using our wide array of electronic gadgets, candle questioning, and so on. When the spirit is *not* making itself known, we are often wasting our time investigating at all. If the spirit's not around at the moment, whether it's gone off somewhere or simply isn't interested at communicating with us, then we have to make an effort. We can try talking and asking questions and so on, but presumably if the spirit is there, it knows we're trying to make contact because we showed up with a load of equipment at the behest of the homeowner. If the spirit knows we're there, and doesn't want to talk, then no amount of shouting or questioning is likely to help.

I've seen sometimes that teams will make an effort to *agitate* a spirit into responding. The team will deliberately do things the spirit doesn't like with the hope of making the spirit upset enough that it lashes out. They often then try to reverse course once the spirit has successfully been agitated into showing itself, "just asking questions" or pretending to be friendly. This is hardly convincing to a person, surely it's not convincing to a spirit; least of all when such a spirit may possess some degree of telepathy. Even the stupidest animals will not trust someone after being hit, at least not easily. So, I propose a friendly, congenial approach with magic. Making offerings, performing peaceful conjurations (perhaps more correctly called invitations), and genuinely approaching the spirit in a way that is non-hostile and friendly is much, much more likely to get us the result we want.

The other consideration is that because many of the conventional means of spirit communication are exhausting for spirits, it is better to provide a means of communication that is very easy to use. Many divination techniques can easily be used here. I've mentioned already pendulum dowsing and candle questioning, and would also propose simply resting the mind, observing what thoughts come, and looking for thoughts that are obviously not one's own. This requires a lot of training usually, as it is difficult both to quiet our own mind as well as to prevent ourselves from thinking ourselves whatever we think the spirit might be thinking. For this reason, if this telepathic approach to spirit communication is intended, I strongly recommend *against* doing research ahead of time, as it will be very easy to imagine up the kinds of thoughts we think the ghost of a girl who died in a fire, or whatever, might well communicate to us.

In terms of general approach, I find the best method is to simply assume that the experiences are reported are true and accurate and work with that. A lot of time, energy, and effort is often expended trying to verify the claims of the paranormal. A lot of work is done ruling out claims, finding potential, non-paranormal reasons for the experiences, and so on. In many cases, this is in fact what the affected person wants. They don't believe in the paranormal or the occult, and so would rather have their claims "debunked," and have evidence found that supports their strictly scientific view that all of this kind of thing is fictional. This is a perfectly find approach, but we don't need occult or psychic methods to do this. There are a great number of skeptical resources available that would be better for that purpose.

Rather than focus on the idea of debunking or trying to prove the haunting authentic, a better approach is to take things as they present themselves. Should, in the course of the investigation, evidence present itself that there is no haunting, or that there are other explanations that are perhaps more consistent with consensus reality, then that should be noted. But we needn't concern ourselves too much with going out of our way to prove things one way or the other. Instead, treat paranormal investigations less like scientific research and more like criminal investigations. Leave the discussion of whether ghosts or hauntings or so on are real to the scientists and philosophers to argue with heavy burdens of proof, and instead focus our efforts on the reported experiences of real people. We would not be very happy if, having called the police to report a burglary, they first started debating whether property exists at all, or if burglaries can even happen, or whether the property was mine in the first place. We would not be satisfied until they set these discussions aside and started looking at the problem we have presented. Similarly, *except when it is the stated intent*, a haunted person rarely calls for a paranormal investigator or ghost hunter or priest or sorcerer for the purpose of proving to them whether or not hauntings are real. They want information or, more likely, resolution to a problem that they already *know* is real. After all, if they didn't believe a ghost or spirit was responsible, and if they thought it was an issue with their duct work, they would have already called an HVAC repairman. If that had resolved their issue, then they wouldn't have taken the step of calling a paranormal investigator. The paranormal already exists far enough outside our social consensus that overcoming the stigma has already required an extraordinary amount of evidence for the afflicted person. And, if they called a paranormal investigator *first*, then they are unlikely to be interested in quibbling over whether or not hauntings are real. For those reasons, I suggest we skip it and move on to brass tacks.

Having established the tools of the ghost hunt or the paranormal investigation, and ruled out the demonstration of the existing of a haunting as the goal, the time has come to ask: why we would do this at all? There are many reasons for investigating the paranormal beyond legend tripping or personal satisfaction. The most important of these, I would argue, is to alleviate the suffering and confusion of people who are experiencing the haunting. The simple truth is, ghost hunters are called by real people experiencing real, confusing, and sometimes frightening things. Generally, these people will not be satisfied if a ghost hunter comes and says, "Welp, yes, you certainly are being haunted, Mrs. Smith. That will be $100." Or, worse, "We found no evidence of a haunting," with the implication of "*your experiences are false and invalid.*" Nobody wants to hear this! And it's not useful. You might say that it's not about what they *want* to hear, and that's fair. I am certainly *not* saying ghost hunters or paranormal investigators should impugn themselves by falsely reporting they have found things when they did not, just to please the client. But of course, absence of evidence is not evidence of absence, and all that. Failing to find evidence doesn't mean a person imagined the whole thing. *They* certainly don't think they did. So instead, I like to focus paranormal investigation not on *proving a haunting* but rather on *providing remediation*. Gathering evidence, performing investigations, and so on is an important first step, but it's merely a first step in the process of *remediation*. Before we commit to solving a haunting, after all, we'd do well to seek out the cause of the complaint, to gather information, and to provide that information to the affected person. But that's not a solution to the problem. That only confirms the problem exists. Instead of stopping there, we should ask, "What can we do with this information?"

An Introduction to Subtle Energy Work

There are any number of magico-religious approaches to dealing with spirits. Of these, one of the most popular, at least around the turn of the last century, was the Spiritualist approach of psychic mediumship. For a number of reasons, this approach fell out of popularity. Spiritualists generally believed they were contacting the spirits of deceased persons, for example; though we have already discussed that in most cases this does not seem to be the case. Instead, spirits tend to be sentient beings with their own unique consciousnesses, rather than the enduring consciousness of a deceased person. Nevertheless, it's certain that spirits are in the world and comprised of some kind of subtle energy. This energy cannot be detected through any known measurement device, though its *effects* in the world can be.

Parapsychology, the study of anomalous phenomena under which psychic research is conducted, moved away from Spiritualism in the early 1900s, as a number of prominent psychic mediums at the time were demonstrated to be frauds when under scrutiny. There are a number of reasons that contributed to this, including, well, fraud. In many cases a pressure to conduct increasingly visually impressive séances in order to impress guests led even legitimate mediums to engage in deceptive practices to add to the experience generally. Well-paying clients did not want a few answers to some questions, to hear that there was a land spirit nearby, or especially to hear that nothing in particular was interested in conversing at the time. Sitters at séances wanted ectoplasm, physical manifestations, and eerie, inexplicable occurrences. Because a medium who could not produce these phenomena would soon be put out of business by a medium (or fraud) who *did,* and because it was particularly profitable to produce these kinds of effects, fraud became rampant. Legitimate parapsychologists in turn moved away from Spiritualism, and while research on the endurance of the consciousness after death continues even today within the field, parapsychologists have for the most part focused on other anomalous phenomena.

Among these other topics are the performance of psychic abilities, including telepathy (direct thought transference), empathy (direct emotion transference), and clairvoyance (the ability to see things at a distance through psychic means). For many years parapsychologists focused on demonstrating the reality of these abilities under laboratory conditions. Today, most parapsychological research is process oriented, aimed at discovering more about the nature and properties of these psychic abilities.

At the same time, spiritual traditions retain an interest in demonstrating psychic ability. As Spiritualism waned in popularity, the Theosophical Society was on the rise, and while Theosophy stood somewhere between a psychic system, a spiritual system, and a new magico-religious order, its writings have had a prominent role in shaping New Age ideas. Helena Blavatsky's *The Secret Doctrine* went into considerable detail about what essentially constitutes energy working. C.W. Leadbeater's *The Chakras* details aspects of the subtle energy anatomy, borrowed from Hindu Tantric texts. Theosophy, in short, bridged the gap between the Western and Eastern esoteric traditions. Whereas the Western traditions focused on ritual magic for gaining results and attainments, the East had focused on the development of personal power through internal work with meditation and yoga.

Today's energy worker is an inheritor of a modern system based in part on modern innovation and in part on ancient Tantra. The Theosophical model of seven chakras, for example, pervades Western thought about subtle energy, despite being only one model out of many. The model of the energy body developed by theosophists relates to planes previously identified in Hermetic texts, though it draws connections to chakras which are only present in certain relatively modern Tantras. Nothing, in short, is clear.

Subtle energy work, however, is useful to us in working with spirits because it provides a vehicle by which we can sense and interact with spirits. Where the paranormal investigator is unable to detect a spirit, the psychic is able to draw it out and encourage it to engage with the investigators. This requires no extra tools or props and no particular knowledge of the spirits beforehand. By the same token, these skills require far more extensive training and practice to use reliably. Because we are not relying on empirical tools to detect the spirit, we have to be more confident in our capabilities, and we must take additional steps to avoid deluding ourselves. Far worse than any fraud we could commit against others is fraud we commit against ourselves and believe to be true. We must take extraordinary precautions to avoid this.

PRELIMINARY EXERCISES: MEDITATION AND AWARENESS

Though there are a number of different methods for teaching psychic ability and intuition development, most of them are comprised of similar elements. According to a review conducted by Emily Sadowski, New Age self-help books, a broad category in which she includes everything from works by Belleruth Naparstek to those by W.E. Butler in the 70s and 80s, all include at the least meditation, imaginative play, and attention exercises. While different texts may have their own methods for the specific performance of skills, these three elements are critical to their foundations. For example, Butler details methods for clairvoyance including waterbowl gazing and for telepathy in conditions that are fairly rigorous, but recognizes the essential need for a meditative foundation. Naparstek includes a number of very overt imaginative play exercises in the form of her guided imagery.

If we want to be successful in developing our psychic faculties to sense, communicate, and interact with spirits, we need to first practice meditation. This isn't because meditation itself is somehow a secret to unlocking cognitive power, though it does have a number of benefits in our daily lives. Instead, the purpose of this meditation is to train our mind. Butler suggests that the goal of the psychic is not to gain access to some information nobody else has. We all have intuition and the potential for extrasensory perception. Instead, the challenge is bringing psychic impressions from the unconscious mind to the conscious mind. Because our minds are so often occupied, this task is not easy. Additionally, meditation can give us insight into how our own minds and the world function that we would not otherwise have. Essentially, we're able to notice much subtler things in our surroundings when our mind is quieted and not in the habit of looking for things to occupy itself with. Far more important than anything which activates some kind of dormant psychic sense, we have to create the conditions in ourselves that allow our intuitions to blossom into conscious awareness.

Historically, meditation is known as a way to develop psychic ability and intuition in and of itself. The Buddha cautioned his monks against engaging in public displays of *siddhis*, or miracle powers, because they can lead to distraction from the path. The Hindu yogi Patanjali taught that *siddhis* can be attained through the recitation of mantras, through rituals, or through *Samadhi*, or meditative accomplishment. But this is not the goal of our meditation, as this process requires in depth instruction under a guru and considerable time. While these abilities naturally fruit as the result of meditative attainment, the other spiritual benefits of that level of practice would far outweigh them anyhow. Instead, our meditation is much simpler, and is intended only to help tame the mind and bring about conditions conducive to intuition development.

Mindfulness

The first step here will be to calm the mind. There is nothing special required for the practice of meditation. We do not need yoga pants or a fancy cushion or the transmission of powerful mantras. All we need is our own body and a little time. Generally, there are seven aspects to the meditative posture, but we only need to concern ourselves with two of them right now. First, it's important that we have a stable posture, where our body is not unsteady or tense. This is the reason many meditation teachers teach the lotus position, with a firm and flat foundation under the body. However, this posture can take many months of practice to master easily, and in some cases it's not possible for people to sit like this. Fortunately, the posture itself, while exceptionally stable, isn't inherently necessary. Instead, we can sit on a chair with our feet planted firmly on the ground. Or, we can sit crosslegged, so long as the back and hips are attended to. If you can manage a lotus posture or have a meditation cushion and know the correct postures, by all means you should use those, but the most important thing is that your body is both stable and relaxed.

Second, we need to have a straight back. This does not mean the *spine* should be straight, but rather simply that the head should be positioned above the hips without the back being slouched. It is enough that we sit upright with our shoulders slightly back. We should pay attention to our hips and make sure that they are aligned upright. Many Westerners are in the habit of sitting with their hips rolled back slightly, which forces the lower back into a curve and causes discomfort and instability. So we should pay attention that our back is straight without significant curvature at the hips, that our head is mostly upright, and that our shoulders are back. The hands can then be placed on the knees or in the lap.

With this posture in mind, we can begin actually meditating in what is called calm-abiding meditation. For this calm-abiding meditation, we need a focal object. This can be a physical thing, like a pebble, a candle flame, or so on, or it can be an intangible thing like the breath. Many meditators prefer the breath because it is something that is always with us, which is relatively constant, and which goes in obvious cycles. When we have selected an object, we simply want to rest the mind on it. This means that we should hold the object in our mind without analyzing it or intentionally thinking about it. If we are focusing on our breathing, for example, we should notice it, but we do not need to count it or think in words "I am breathing in, I am breathing out." This can help to begin with, but we should eventually move to simply recognizing it without labeling it in words.

Resting the mind like this will at first usually cause many distracting thoughts to pop up. Our minds are in the habit of thinking all sorts of things, and when left idle it looks for things to think about. Whenever we notice our mind has wandered, we should acknowledge whatever it is that came up, and then return to the focal object. We will notice thoughts, feelings, and even physical sensations constantly arising. It is easy to get discouraged at this stage! But we should remember that the recognition of these thoughts, feelings, and sensations is actually a success. Every time we recognize our own distraction and return to the focal object, we are training our minds not to wander but instead to rest without grasping for new things.

We shouldn't try to meditate for too long at first. Many people think that meditation should take twenty minutes or an hour or more. Stereotypes tell us that we should spend many days in long meditations. In fact, it's far better that we meditate for a short time successfully than for a long time with many distractions. Whenever we feel that there is something we absolutely must attend to, or that we just cannot rest the mind on the breath or other object, then we should stop meditating at that point. If we're lifting weights at the gym, and the weight is too heavy for us to lift, we do not benefit much from straining against it. In fact, we can hurt ourselves! The same is true here: we should meditate for as long as we're able, but not try to force ourselves to meditate longer. I usually suggest we start as short as one minute. If that one minute passes so easily that we are never distracted during it, then we should try for five minutes. If on the other hand we are restless and cannot meditate even for one minute, then try for thirty seconds. Even thirty second's meditation, if really good, will be more beneficial than thirty minutes of distracted meditation that makes us angry and discouraged.

Just Noticing

After we've practiced this for a few days and are comfortable with it, the next stage is to notice the distractions that enter our mind but, instead of immediately cutting them and returning to the reference object as we did during mindfulness, we should label them and identify them. We do not want to indulge them or follow them too closely! We don't want to find ourselves hungry, identify hunger, and then begin thinking about lunch. This is not meditation, then, but rather just following our established hunger. Instead, we should look more deeply at it. We've labeled it hunger, so what is hunger *like*? What are the individual sensations that arise in the guts? What is the mental state? Is it frantic or calm? Stressed or relaxed? Do we feel this hunger just in our stomach? Or is it in our shoulders? Our arms and legs? What does it feel like there?

We can perform this exercise wherever we are, at any time, but it requires that we first have the discipline of mindfulness. If we can't maintain our focus without analysis on a focal object, then any attempt to look deeper at phenomena will be cut short. We won't notice the more subtle qualities and characteristics of how we feel. Our usual habit is to notice that we feel a certain way and then follow from that point to another point. We recognize, for example, that we're hungry, so we begin thinking about food. We see that we're tired, so we begin thinking about bed. All sorts of emotions start to arise, but we can't even tell them apart necessarily. Therapists often teach their clients to build a more robust emotional vocabulary, because our general habit is to use deficient, simple emotional words. Are we "mad?" Or are we indignant? Frustrated? Perturbed? Annoyed? Can we even differentiate those for ourselves? When we meditate by just noticing, we stay with these emotions and other states, rather than rushing to pacify them, to see their more subtle characteristics.

Meditation for Energy Work

Like with emotions, we don't really have a fantastic vocabulary for describing psychic impressions. When we receive information intuitively, or through psychometry, or through telepathy or so on, we have to experience these within our own bodies and minds. As a result, we often cannot make sense of it on its own, and we have to map these impressions to other existing perceptual channels. Subtle energy does not actually push on our skin, but we might feel a pressure. It is not actually warm or cool, but we feel warmth or coldness. In some cases, when investigating spirits, we will notice hot and cold spots. Often this is understood to be a result of a spirit drawing energy from the environment, but we know that subtle energy does not have thermodynamic properties. However, subtle energy does impress itself onto the environment just as the environment impresses itself onto subtle energy fields. These cold spots can be understood as the physical world reshaping itself to accommodate energetic fields. We could be intersecting the spirit and noticing its energy as cold, and a thermometer that detects this cold spot could be accommodating that perception as the actual world shapes to accommodate the energetic world. Or, this could be an attempt at communication, with the spirit exercising subtle influence to allow us to notice its presence.

In any case, what is important to recognize is that subtle energy is often felt as a physical sensation, but without a physical cause. These perceptions come from our mind interpreting subtle, psychic information through a sensory channel that is comprehensible to us. We have practiced mindfulness and just noticing in meditation in order to heighten our sensitivity to these sensations, so that we can recognize them when they occur. In our usual distracted way of thinking, we might notice for a moment we are slightly colder, adjust our jacket, and that would be the end of it. We might feel a sudden emotion arise, then cast about for a reason we feel that way. If we are not paying attention, we may not notice at all the disruption in our internal monologue that indicates a spirit is attempting to impress its thoughts onto us in order to communicate. Once we have mastered these very basic meditations, however, our capacity for sensing subtle energy changes will be greatly expanded. Now comes the task of identifying what they *mean*.

The Energy Body and Spirits

As discussed before, we cannot detect subtle energy through any standard instruments or physical means. How we can detect subtle energy is through subtle energy. Our own body consists not only of the physical aspect, but also of subtle elements as well. The Theosophical Society termed these other bodies the etheric and astral bodies. The physical body is what we generally think of when we say "our body" and refers to the material flesh and blood that exists in the physical world. The etheric body overlays this physical body, conditions it, and is conditioned by it. It extends for about three to twelve inches off of the surface of our physical body, and reflects the general health and status of our body. When we feel well, we imprint that good feeling onto the etheric body. When we feel sick, we imprint the etheric field corresponding to that part of the body onto the etheric body as well. When our etheric body is harmed, this is reflected in our physical feelings of wellbeing. Enduring energetic harm can lead to the manifestation of physical illnesses.

Just as the etheric body reflects our physical state, the astral body reflects our mental state—our thoughts, emotions, and intents. It expands and contracts based on our mental wellbeing and balance, and its characteristics are similarly representative. When we are angry, our astral body may flare and animate, and while we are sad, it may shrink and become dull and stagnant. Where the etheric and astral fields overlap is usually what people are referring to when they talk about a person's "aura," though the astral body can be as small as the etheric body or as expansive as 20 feet, or in some meditative states even infinitely expansive.

Of course, we're not the only beings with bodies like this. Spirits similarly have etheric and astral bodies, with similar properties, though generally without a physical body to serve as the coarse anchor we have. What this means is that spirits struggle to interact with the physical world directly. We can flip a light switch using our hand for minimal effort, a spirit would need to expend considerable effort to psychokinetically flip a switch, provided the spirit even knows how to accomplish such a feat. It is a mistake to assume that spirits are born with an innate knowledge of how to interact with the physical world. These are learned skills for spirits as well as for us. However, because spirits consist of etheric and astral bodies as we do, they tend to be very capable of communicating through those bodies. In this case, it is we embodied individuals who neglect the communication, because we do not know how to pay attention to the impressions on our etheric and astral bodies. In short, our etheric and astral senses are generally poor and rarely gain our attention as our minds are so preoccupied with physical sensations.

The process of energy sensation is straightforward: the astral body intersects with the energetic fields of other things and people, including spirits. This creates an impression on the astral field, which in turn creates an impression in the etheric body. All of this happens beneath our awareness, in the unconscious mind. To bring it to the level of conscious awareness, we have to pay attention to it. We make this easier by entering a light trance or meditative state, and further by learning how these impressions will be experienced in the physical body. This last step has already begun if you've been performing the "just noticing" exercises. These exercises do not only represent internal states, but also external impressions. If you have been practicing diligently, at this point you can likely notice subtle differences depending on *where* you meditate. Churches feel different from graveyards which feel different from crossroads and so on. Depending on people we are around, we can notice different feelings, including emotions and thoughts, even physical maladies in some cases.

However, because each of our energetic bodies changes based on our physical and mental state, the way this information comes into our conscious awareness differs from one person to another. Where I might feel magnetic pressure, another person might feel heat or cold, and still another person might feel tingling or rubbing. These perceptions are just a way of our mind mapping subtle energy sensations into our physical sphere of awareness. Sometimes we may not feel anything at all, instead just knowing intuitively what the state of things is. In any case, we have to strive for internal consistency in perceptions; we cannot compare our impressions to someone else's impressions and assume that this is adequate. In many cases, two different people can be in the presence of the same spirit and have two different perceptions. Neither is *wrong*; both are simply mapping things in their own way based on the state of their own energy body. If we do not establish a vocabulary for our impressions and take notes to maintain consistency, it can take a very long time before we're familiar enough to gain anything useful out of our perceptions.

The skill of detecting and discerning the subtle energies around us is called *psychometry*, and we influence other subtle energies through a process called *imprinting* or *programming.*

PSYCHOMETRY, IMPRINTING, SYMPATHY, AND ANTIPATHY

We know spirits have their own qualities and characteristics, both observable through their behaviors and defining their energetic characteristics. But how can we identify spirits and communicate with them using the skills discussed so far? The practice of psychometry comes into play here. Psychometry is often associated with the gathering of information off a physical object via psychic means. The psychometrist can read the energy connected to, for example, a watch or a phone or a piece of jewelry, and possibly report information about the owner. There are a number of factors which complicate this, however. Psychic information comes to us just as any other sensory information does, as a block or jumble that we sort out into useful fragments and organize into meaningful information. It's entirely possible for two people with the same sensitivity to give wildly different reports of essentially the same information. The quality of delivery, the organization, and the acuity of the information are all things moderated not by the psychometrist's psychic sensitivity, but by his or her general communicative and thinking skills. The previous exercises have hopefully served to help us organize the information we receive into meaningful pieces. The ability to organize descriptions of our normal senses and to notice subtler details rather than being blinded by the whole image taken together.

There's no reason, however, that we should limit our ability to read these subtle energies to the reading of physical objects. Just as with a phone or watch, we can apply the same methods of gathering information to spirits. The information we receive will come in much the same way, and is the product of the conscious mind "unpacking" the information encoded into a spirit's field the same way we might make assumptions about a person we pass on the street based on his or her gait, clothing, mannerisms, and so further. We may receive any number of physical sensory information: colors, memories of sounds, physical reactions, and on and on. These can come in many forms and in many cases represent personal symbolism more so than actual characteristics of the spirit. After all, the spirit has no color and no need for it, as color is a property of light and not of spirit. However, depending on our own culture, that color may be our own mind's way of encoding information. Red, for example, might represent anger or evil, or just as soon it may represent auspiciousness and good fortune and generosity, depending on your upbringing. It is very rare that the spirit will willingly project information of this symbolic nature, though not impossible.

The converse of psychometry is *imprinting*, the act of charging an object or area with information we provide. Just as our energy body is receptive to impressions, our field leaves impressions on other things. Through an act of deliberate will we can focus our own thoughts and intentions onto other objects or locations. When hauntings occur that aren't the result of spirits, this is usually the culprit. In the previous section we discussed haunted houses which have become haunted by way of a person having a highly emotional event in the area, or being the victim of violence, or whatever else. These emotional extremes impress themselves onto the environment in a moment what normally takes significant time to mold. Jewelry or other personal effects may carry a person's information on them due to many months or years of contact with the person's energy field, but the same quality and strength of impression can be achieved by a particularly powerful impression being made all at once. This will be something we return to in several later sections, as it is the basis by which sympathetic or antipathetic qualities are imprinted onto areas, the means by which telepathic concepts can be communicated, and a method of harmonization that allows for channeling. While it doesn't seem that all telepathic communication is related to energy directly, this foundation of psychometry and imprinting can serve to reproduce a substantial number of psychic effects.

The most common uses for deliberate imprinting in working with spirits are in shaping the environment to attract or repel spirits by impressing qualities on the environment that they like or dislike. We can attract spirits to come to us by projecting energy with a quality they like into the environment around us. Conversely, we can induce a spirit to lash out in frustration, or potentially drive it away entirely, by imprinting the environment with qualities it dislikes. In both cases this can be accomplished through creating imprints. We passively imprint our thoughts and ideas onto the environment all the time, unless we take deliberate precautions to avoid this. However, this generally takes time and is not particularly strong. In many cases of hauntings focused on people, it is some mental or physical quality of the person reflected in the energy body that creates sympathy which attracts the spirit, or else some disliked feature that agitates the spirit into trying to drive the person away.

One of the main tools for imprinting energy is visualization. First, we need to bring to mind what it is we want to imprint. For example, we might want to imprint an environment with energy like that of children playing. So we need to bring to mind children playing, and try to invoke the same feelings, thoughts, ideas and experiences in ourselves. We can then visualize these feelings as an energy, gathering within our body, and then visualize it flowing into the object. Visualization in this case serves to instruct our unconscious mind to push the energy accordingly. We're intentionally pushing, in this case, and not relying on the passive effect mentioned before—though that would work, given enough time. Visualization is a tool, and in itself only has a very limited effect of directing the astral body. Any act of directing our will can work for this task. We can simply push with our mind, for example.

It is also possible to produce protective effects that keep spirits away or attract a spirit with simply that intent, and no knowledge of the spirit's sympathies or antipathies. This can be less precise, however, and slightly more difficult to hold such an intent in our mind. The more specific an idea, the easier it is to focus. More vague ideas are slightly harder to hold in the mind and project. When possible, we should try to be more specific unless we are deliberately trying to accomplish a range of effects.

Until this point, we have most likely been focusing on performing psychometry or imprinting by holding an object in our hand or while standing in the same room. However, it's also possible to achieve these effects at a distance. The astral body moves with thought, and we can project a "tendril" of our thoughts out to touch objects remotely, even at great distance and with seemingly no signal degradation. These tendrils can be used to both psychometrize and imprint upon objects remotely. Maintaining them is a matter of the same visualization and intention. It is even possible, as we'll discuss later regarding clairvoyance, to ascertain information about unknown objects through remote psychometry.

Energetic Self-Defense and Self-Care

Because we influence and are influenced by the environment around us, it is necessary that we take precautions for our own security when we are working with potentially hostile spirits. Even in our daily lives, once we have attained a degree of sensitivity, it often makes sense to temporarily suppress these senses than to go about unlearning everything we have learned in order to achieve that psychic ability. To that end, there are a number of measures we can employ. Most common among these are the use of shields and protective fields. These are constructs built by first shaping the subtle energy around us, and then imprinting it with characteristics that are beneficial to us. For example, a person might surround themselves with energy in the shape of a large egg and then imprint this energy such that it serves as a barrier to keep out other energy or prevent the interaction of two fields. Or, one might create a field of energy that is impassible to certain kinds of spirits. These kinds of defensive measures can be used to help others as well.

The other concern from this influence is the possibility of illness or injury as a result of energetic effects. As discussed before, the physical body is intimately related to the etheric body. Damage or unwellness in one is apparent in the other. This road goes both ways: not only does sickness cause disturbances in the energy field; energetic disturbances can also cause sickness in the physical body. Many spirits will use this directly as a means to drive people away, and we often see this in haunting scenarios where the spirit believes it is entitled to the property which the victim of the haunting has recently moved into. Additionally, some spirits will deliberately cause sickness because they feed on the energy that comes from sickness.

Far more dangerous, however, than physical injury or illness resultant from energetic exposure is the risk of psychological disturbance. The astral field is far more readily shaped, and it is well within the capacity of most spirits to cause psychological harm via energetic manipulation. The physical body provides a protective element to the etheric field: while it's possible for etheric influences to harm it, the body itself is constantly applying a kind of resilience to outside interference. On the other hand, the mind is usually far less stable. Meditation itself helps this substantially, and there is protection in being able to observe and monitor our own thoughts dispassionately, which allows us to recognize external influences. Many young natural telepaths and empaths are caused considerable distress by not being able to differentiate their own thoughts from someone else's, but the experienced meditator can recognize these external influences when they come. Simple awareness of the possibility can provide a protective element.

This is not a perfect defense, however. In the heat of the moment, it can be easy to lose our stability and fall into negative patterns of thinking, especially when we are being influenced by malicious entities. For spirits, this kind of energetic manipulation is their primary means of communication with the physical world, and so they tend to be fairly skilled at it. Deliberate attempts to cause disturbance or traumatic stress are a real threat, especially from spirits that mean us harm. Even the most experienced psychic medium can be harmed by this malicious contact. But other dangers exist. Just as a telepath or empath can be disturbed by contact with individuals who are angry, traumatized, or so on, it's possible that the psychic medium can encounter spirits who are profoundly unwell or otherworldly to an extent that they can disturb our contact with reality.

To this point we've also only spoken of relatively passive contacts, where the spirit is harming the person from outside. These risks are even greater when engaging in channeling, mediumship, or invocation, where we have brought the spirit in and encouraged it to communicate by taking some degree of control over our body. Such an intimate connection of medium and control provides ample opportunity for a spirit to cause significant harm. In rare cases, the spirit will not surrender the body, in which case the channeling becomes a possession and must be exorcised.

There are, of course, ways to defend from this that range from the passive to the extremely active. The first and most important element is that of energetic self-care.

Self-Care

The first and most important element of self-care starts with our physical bodies. Our minds cannot be stable enough to resist malign influence if we are not taking care of ourselves physically. Getting enough sleep, eating good and nutritious meals, exercising and keeping the body well are necessary components of any kind of self-care routine. Resisting influences to the etheric field that can harm the physical body is far easier if the physical body is already healthy. Conversely, it's trivial to cause sickness when that sickness is already made more likely through a weakened immune system or malnourishment. We should not think that because the potential harm that comes from spirits is often energetic in origin, we can get away with only focusing on energetic health to the neglect of our physical health. Similarly, maintaining our mental health is important. It is difficult enough to traffic with spirits and psychic powers in cultures where the paranormal is not already accepted. We do not need to compound internal and external judgment about paranormal beliefs with legitimate concerns about mental health. Taking care of our mental health needs is paramount. This should include good mental hygiene and attempts at maintaining habits of positive thinking, and in cases of mental illness, seeking appropriate medical care. All of this, however, is something you can best learn from other sources.

For maintaining our own energetic health, there are a handful of skills that are important and which can make for a daily routine that is neither time consuming nor resource intensive. Particularly, cleaning, grounding, and centering the energetic field are universally beneficial skills that also serve to increase our resilience against psychic attack, be it from spirits or otherwise.

Let us first discuss grounding and centering. Essentially, these are both methods of reducing external influences on the energy body, essentially "resetting" it to be correspondent to our basic mental and physical bodies. Grounding is a method of dumping energy out of the energy body into the earth in order to stabilize the field. At its most basic, we need only stand with our feet firmly on the ground and mentally "push" energy downward, allowing the field to surge and pulse with energy from the body. We can be a bit more elaborate however for better results.

First, go outside, or if inside, to a place that has been thoroughly cleaned and is energetically neutral. Standing with both feet on the ground at roughly shoulder length apart, in a relaxed posture, take a few deep breaths. Rest your awareness on your energy field. Then, breathing in, visualize the field contracting in tightly around you. Breathing out, see the energy push down into the earth out of the left foot. Then, breathing in, see clean, fresh energy from the earth rise up and enter the energetic field through the right foot. As the energy enters the earth, it is scrubbed of any external influences, and even influences from our own mental state or physical illness. As we breathe in, pure, clean energy comes back into the field. Continue this process, seeing our own energy leaving the body into the earth and feeling this clean, unprogrammed energy refilling the field until the entire field is new, fresh, and unimprinted. This new energy has no negative imprinting or impressions from its surroundings because it is coming from the earth, which is too large and homogenous to be imprinted.

In some cases, it won't be possible, practical, or convenient to go outside. So long as our visualization is firm, however, it is possible to create this loop. Even in a very high building, there is pure, clean earth if we go deep enough. Because energy does not degrade over distance, it is possible to create this cleansing, purifying channel no matter where we are. While I have instructed here to do this in an energetically clean area, it can even be accomplished in a haunted building full of malign influence by someone competent to create those channels and secure them against external influence, although for beginners it should be practiced with as many advantages as possible.

Next, we can practice centering, which essentially attunes the energy in the field back to "us" and so removes external influences through programming. Here, we again want to draw the energy field inward. Ground if possible, to remove as many influences as possible. Relax the body by tensing and relaxing muscles in sequence. Start by scrunching the toes, holding them for about five seconds, then releasing them. Continue to the calves, then the thighs, tensing, counting to five, and relaxing. Tighten the core, then the chest. Pull the shoulders back, then stretch the arms and relax. Ball your hands tightly into fists, count to five, then relax. Continue this process until the entire body has been tensed and relaxed. Then, rest the mind on the body. Allow yourself to feel how your body feels. Notice the feelings, emotions, sensations, and so on in the body. Now, visualize the energetic field aligning itself to these feelings. Influences outside the body are no longer reflected in the field, and the field reflects how the body is now, in the relaxed state. Allow the field to expand naturally as it corresponds with the physical body and mind. Allow the astral body to expand naturally, noticing the thoughts and emotions that enter the mind as it expands and dismissing those which seem related to the environment and which don't reflect the inner calm.

This exercise brings our energetic field into accord with our physical and mental state. It quite obviously should not be practiced when our physical body is unwell or our mind is disturbed, as this will enter a loop that reinforces those conditions. In those scenarios, we should take the opposite tack, visualizing our field as it should be without that illness or disturbance, and pushing that projection of the natural, undisturbed state onto the energy field instead. We can achieve this by visualizing a core of energy at the base of the body, roughly where the weight rests when sitting cross-legged. In the Theosophical Chakra model, this is the root chakra, which connects the etheric body to the physical body. Visualize the energy here expanding and "unpacking" in its natural, organic state. Whatever physical maladies one has, these are not present. Next, repeat this process from an energy center about 3 inches, or four finger lengths, under the navel. This is the "sacral" chakra, and connects the physical body to the emotional aspect of the astral body. This unpacking process restores the emotional state to its natural resting form. Finally, repeat this process again at from an energy center at the solar plexus. This will reset the astral body where it corresponds to the mind.

These chakras shouldn't be considered to be organs of an energetic anatomy, but rather conceptual tools which we use for working with the energy body. This format of chakras was presented in the West first by C.W. Leadbeater in *The Chakras* and based on a relatively late tantric text. In general, chakras are meditative tools used in tantric yoga to train our minds and induce certain results, as we're using them here. If you prefer, this exercise can be condensed by visualizing a single energetic center at the location of the sacral chakra mentioned above which unpacks all three components of the energetic body (the etheric, and the emotional and mental astral).

The previous two exercises can help remove external and mental influences from the energy body. However, sometimes energy can also congest around the field, causing stagnation. This is something we can observe in places especially, where the dynamics of a place will lead to stagnant energy blocking flow. Disciplines such as Chinese *feng shui* are often applied to sustain the flow of energy through places. When this energy congests around the energy body it can dampen our sensitivity. Just like a shield can be a semi-solid construct that prevents energy exchange, energetic detritus in the environment can dampen energetic exchange. When this happens it can result in diminished sensitivity, mental sluggishness, and other deleterious effects.

Fortunately, cleaning this energy is fairly straightforward. We can use incenses, "smudging," and similar methods, which many ritual traditions depend on. However, manually cleaning the field can be done by "rattling" and "scraping." Rattling is simply the use of a rattle around the energy body, about 4 inches or so from the skin, from the top of the head down to the feet, which "breaks up" some of the detritus. Then, using the hand, one can scrape this energy off. It can help to keep the hand rigid and tense, though this isn't strictly necessary.

So that it isn't kept around, we can either ground it, using the same visualization exercise as above while "holding" the energy in the hand, or we can deposit it into a material that absorbs energy, such as salt, and then throw the salt away. We can also dispose of it into running water, such as a drain. A similar effect to rattling can be accomplished simply through taking a shower, and so the entire cleaning, grounding, and centering exercise can be accomplished during a regular shower with little disruption to our daily routine. It can also be supplemented into one's preparations both before and after visiting a haunted location, so as to improve our sensitivity initially and make sure we do not carry energy of the site with us to our own homes.

Shields

Of course, these routines are passive, and will not protect us from a deliberate influence. To achieve this, we need to return to the shield. To create a shield that wards off influence actively, and thus prevent a spirit from deliberately affecting us directly (as can happen if we become the subject of the haunting), we will again return to visualizations. Here, we want to pattern and shape energy. It can be helpful to use our physical hands for this purpose, as it creates a stronger impression in our minds and, in turn, in the energy we're shaping. However, this isn't strictly necessary. For the purposes of protecting ourselves from outside influence, I consider the shield in the form of a hazardous materials suit, encapsulating myself entirely and extending about 12 to 24 inches off of my physical form. The reason for this is that I want to include the entire etheric body as well as the astral body inside the shield. This shield is then seen as keeping a strict separation between my energy body and surrounding energy fields. It can allow me to reach out via a tendril, to sense the area around me, but does not allow influences to pass beyond that point without my awareness. The visualizations here are something we should develop ourselves. Many authors provide visualizations, including constructing the shield out of stone bricks to create a "stone tower" around oneself, or building a sphere of energy around oneself seen as glowing shielding like in a movie. However, what is important about visualization is that we are setting our minds in motion to shape energy according to our conscious will. Using other visualizations may not communicate the symbolism of what we intend strongly enough. By using our own inner symbolism, we increase our ability to shape and imprint energy. To achieve this, we can return to meditation, where we should now consider topics deeply, looking at all of the internal symbols that arise as we journey inward. This process can take considerable time, but will be of inestimable benefit, not only for visualization, but for uncovering our own internal realities and how we interact with the world through symbols and hidden meanings.

There are unfortunately no magic bullet solutions to spiritual dangers. Energetic harm can happen despite our best precautions, and these defensive techniques are not sufficient to deal with every threat we might encounter. Though we inhabit the same astral realms, most of us have habitually only attended to our physical world. Because we are acculturated and accustomed to the physical world, our etheric and astral natures are often neglected and underdeveloped. Spirits, as etheric and astral beings, have an advantage of familiarity when it comes to energy work that only time and experience can overcome. My other text, *Subtle Energy*, goes into more detail on much of this energy work, but even that would be insufficient to handle many spiritual dangers. We should always be careful to maintain a network of support that can help us when we face spiritual threats, and take care not to agitate spirits unnecessarily through our work. Increased sensitivity comes with increased vulnerability, and while these defensive and self-care techniques can minimize that risk, it cannot remove it. Always have a backup plan when dealing with spirits!

Communication via Energy

One of our main purposes for practicing this kind of subtle energy working in the first place is to establish a route of communication with spirits. Whether we are mediums assisting a paranormal investigation, consultants working to help a client understand the nature of an event, or people living in a haunted house, having a reliable line of communication with a spirit is extremely useful. We can, of course, depend more upon material means of divination, by which a spirit can communicate with us. This is detailed further in section three. In this section, we need only apply what we've already learned.

Psychic communication is generally divided, arbitrarily, into *empathy*, the extrasensory communication of emotions, and *telepathy*, the extrasensory communication of thoughts. I say that this is arbitrary because it is a common sense division and yet there's really little basis for it. Our best understanding of emotion itself is that it comes from our best rationalizations for a given state of physiological arousal.[9] Despite this, there are people who claim to be *solely* telepathic, or, more commonly, *solely* empathic. In most cases, this seems to be a result of their personal psychological disposition. Empathic individuals tend to be more emotional overall, and so they recognize and are more attuned to emotional information. Additionally, emotional information seems to be more readily transmitted simply because it is less complex than thought information. Finally, thought information more often than not is *proto-conceptual.* That is, it has not yet been turned into a conceptual thought, but rather it is the pre-conceptual form of a thought, before it is formed into words. Thus, even telepathic individuals often struggle in telepathy with other people with

---

[9] The two-factor theory of emotion, first proposed by Schachter and Singer in 1962.

whom they are unfamiliar, because the pre-conceptual information is formed into a concept in their own mind, not the mind of the original thinker, and thus it lacks the character of the original thinker's thoughts in most cases.

With all these factors in mind, the division of extrasensory communication into two separate disciplines does not appear to be based in some kind of functional difference, but simply based on individual disposition. Some people are more disposed to interpret emotional information, some more disposed to thought information, and with training both sorts of people can learn to do either. Just as a sports player might have a preferred position, but yet knows the functions of all the positions and in a pinch could probably perform those responsibilities, a psychic is capable of learning all of these skills, though may have strong preferences for some over others based on his or her personal dispositions.

For our purposes, however, I will continue to differentiate them in term if not in function. There is a convention within parapsychology of making this division, and we must work within the language set of the field we're using. New terms, such as "anomalous cognition," more closely correspond to what is actually being observed, but they lack a degree of familiarity and this intentionally sterile language can sometimes be even vaguer than the preconceptions about the established terminology. So, I will continue to refer to "telepathy" and "empathy" distinctly and leave it as a task for the reader to remember that generally speaking these are the same skill.

It is perhaps moot anyhow, as the form of telepathy and empathy we will discuss here relies entirely on psychometry, rather than on some otherwise unknown skill. The mechanisms by which telepathy and empathy function are not known. It is known that the same conditions that lead to their demonstration can also lead to sensitivity to subtle energy. Private experiments among telepaths, empaths, and general intuitives seem to indicate that these skills are distinct from energy sensing and imprinting via the energy body, as we will discuss. But these experiments also make assumptions about the validity of perceptions that I'm unwilling to make. In short, I cannot say with certainty how any form of telepathy or empathy works, but in some cases it does seem to be a distinct skill from the psychometric techniques we will be discussing. In other cases, particularly when the skill is learned intentionally, it seems to be exactly this form of energetic exchange. And because the properties of energy itself are ill understood, it's possible that it's all the same skill in different forms of presentation.

We have already discussed that our energy body is in a constant state of exchange and mutual influence with surrounding energy fields, including those of spirits. And we have discussed how the different layers of the energy body and their relative densities (for lack of a better word) correspond to the emotions and the thoughts of a person. The physical body is the densest and interacts with other physical objects directly. The etheric body overlaps it and relates to it, though exists of more subtle things, and principally relates to sensations. The astral body comes in two densities, one corresponding to emotion, and the other to thought. The bodies themselves are of different sizes and so overlap with different fields.

At its most basic, when the energy body is in contact with the energy body of a spirit, communication is very straightforward. Our body is subtly affected by the thoughts and feelings of the spirit. These are represented to us as a change in our energy body. Because we have practiced meditation and learned to notice these subtle changes in our own body, we can recognize these changes as they occur. Because the spirit is attempting to communicate, these may take the form of thoughts. Whereas many impressions may come in the form of physical sensations in our body, thoughts typically will not. Here it is important that we practice the same meditation as before, but focused on our thoughts. We should look very carefully at them, resting the thinking on our breathing, but now paying attention to where the thoughts begin and end. Our own thoughts have particular qualities we can recognize. They arise and fall in a certain way. There is a recognizable gap between them, from which they arise and back to which they return. The thoughts of spirits, however, will seem slightly different.

For some people, it will be very easy to identify our own thoughts and the thoughts of others as separate. For others, it will be more difficult, or there will initially be an absence of thoughts seemingly originating from others. The difference between these groups really is only initial sensitivity, because all people possess the same capacity for psychic perception. We can liken this to "supertasters," individuals who have a remarkably acute sense of taste. It is not difficult for them to identify subtle differences in flavors because they are naturally more sensitive to those flavors. However, anyone can learn to discern flavors if given enough time and the inclination to do so. In the same way, some people will have a difficult time discerning thoughts, and it will come more easily to others, but in the end the same results can be achieved with practice.

At this point I should take a moment to note the nature of thoughts as they arise. These should not be understood to be like "voices in our head." A voice, the impression that we're actually hearing something, is very different. This is a hallucination, and while it is possible for spirits to cause hallucinations (by injecting the perceptions directly into the thoughts), it is not what we're looking to accomplish here. Instead, these will seem like thoughts, and thoughts they are. The distinction between these thoughts and imagined thoughts will essentially be in the cause that precipitates them. A degree of mental discipline is necessary to make sure we are not attempting to guess at what the spirit would say. When we attempt this, we incline ourselves to imagine what a spirit would think, and we become prone to fantasy. This is needless to say not what we are wanting to accomplish. For this purpose, if the communication is meant in any way to be part of an investigation, the medium should be blind to the target. That is, they should not know anything about the spirit with whom they are communicating prior to the communication beginning.

To achieve this, the medium can be brought to the location of the spirit and asked simply to reach out for communication without any briefing and with attempts made to hide any information that might poison the well, or the medium can work remotely. To target remotely, the spirit might be assigned a name or description which is given to the medium but which does not relate to the spirit's actual nature or to those things known about the spirit. A home address or a person is often enough. If the spirit has been given a name by the haunted people, and there are no other details and the name does not relate to some facet of the case, then this could be used. Essentially, every effort must be taken to prevent the medium from receiving information which would incline him or her to guess at what the spirit might be trying to say, or otherwise to try to "figure out" the communication rather than just receive it. And, the medium must be diligent to monitor him or herself for these processes being in play.

With even a little experience it is rather trivial to differentiate telepathic or empathic impressions from imagined thoughts and feelings. When we *do* find that we are imagining or fantasizing about communication, instead of receiving it cleanly, it is best to take a significant amount of time away from the site and with adequate distractions so that it can be re-approached with a fresh mind. We should also note to ourselves and to whomever is documenting our impressions that this is what we are doing. This deliberate noting in our minds that we are taking a break because we fantasized or imagined is a way of training our own mind not to do this. This is a critical step that is all too often missed and leads to undisciplined mediums who, while sometimes very accurate, will struggle with confidence.

Spirit communications are not often about things that immediately make sense to us. When attempting to communicate with spirits, the thoughts may not organize themselves in a way that seems to make sense. There will often have to be a period of back and forth clarification. The medium should write down thoughts as they come to mind in descriptive, abstract language rather than in concrete formats. At this stage, unless a narrative immediately presents itself, no attempt should be made to organize it into a story. Information can come through in a disjointed, disorganized manner, and will be clarified through impressions. Only after the flow information seems to have stopped should the medium begin trying to piece it together. Ideally, this is done promptly, while on scene, because as the medium attempts to figure things out, the spirit can pay attention and attempt to help clarify things either with more information or by nudging the thoughts of the medium.

Usually, the medium needs to make no particular attempt to communicate, as the spirit will be attuned and listening. However, if the medium does need to emphasize a communication or make an effort to be heard, this can be done by "thinking loudly" and by visualizing the thoughts forming more densely, pulsing or rippling through the energetic field like ripples on the surface of the water. Each "beat" of the thought is like a pebble striking the surface, and the thought is "pulsing" out through the field, shaping it accordingly. If the spirit is known to the medium, or if contact is being made from afar, the same "tendril" visualizations from earlier can be used, and this "pulsing" can be directed down the tendril. Generally, "pulse sending," or thinking the desired thought repeatedly in short bursts, is more effective than trying to hold the thought for a long time or to concentrate on the thought. Typically unless the spirit has already demonstrated that it is listening to thoughts and is willing to interact normally, it is best to use these pulse-sending methods along with short instructions. Far more effective than yelling verbally into the void is persistently "pulsing" an intent in a way that shapes the room.

Empathy with spirits can be a complicated topic simply because so often a spirit's emotions are foreign to our own. Many spirits have extremely long existences. Land owning spirits may exist in a space for thousands of years. While all spirits, like people, essentially want to be happy, they may not place the same value in brief exchanges. Spirits that recognize that a paranormal investigation is likely to be transient and result in little change are unlikely to want to put in the effort to reach out. While some spirits are inclined to have fun along with or at the expense of people, others are markedly disinterested, and it can be difficult to tell which is which.

However, emotions are very commonly used by spirits as forms of defense. A spirit might fill a room with anger, fear, sadness, or so on in order to induce these feelings in human inhabitants. The purposeful induction of negative emotions is a very common method for spirits to defend themselves and attack people. Defending from this is important, as individuals who have honed their sensitivity will be more easily affected. Even though recognizing the cause of the emotion can somewhat offset its power, the emotion arises nevertheless, and it takes a lot of discipline to control one's behavior in such a circumstance. Defending from these kinds of attacks, however, can be as simple as shielding oneself using the methods discussed before. Here, we create a barrier around ourselves (or others!) approximately 2 feet from the surface of the skin which does not allow influence of emotions in or out. This allows us to feel our own emotions, but not to have external inputs affecting the emotional energy body. It is important that we be able to feel our own emotions, because these emotions—fear especially—are important for our survival, especially in strange circumstances. We wouldn't want to miss a gut feeling of danger because we've dampened our own sensitivity. Additionally, emotional responses to spirits are not uncommon, and it's important that we can differentiate between emotional responses that arise in response to encountering a certain type of spirit, and emotional responses that are being induced by that spirit psychically.

Clairvoyance

Yet another application of energy work can be accomplished through these sensitivity exercises we have conducted so far. Clairvoyance is a term with significantly broad scope, but generally refers to either seeing at a distance through extrasensory means, or with seeing spirits directly. Both applications can be developed through strictly energetic routes. Beginning with the familiar, it is not a stretch of the imagination to say that we can learn, with practice, to map the psychic inputs of our psychometric perceptions to spatial locations in the physical world. From here, we can, with practice, begin to *see* the barriers and edges of energetic fields, including the energy bodies of spirits, in the mind's eye. This can require a trance, or for particularly strong inputs, it may appear to use normally. Once again, it is important that we recognize this enough that it does not become a hallucination. Spirits can cause these kinds of visual hallucinations. In most cases where a spirit is appearing physically to someone, unless there is a medium such as fog or smoke that the spirit can manifest within, it is a hallucination. When there is a physical medium that the spirit can use to take shape, then it may sometimes be an actual effect of appearance.

Allan Kardec, the French founder of Spiritism, wrote about the physical transformation of the medium. I strongly suspect that in almost all of these cases, if not all, the effect that was occurring was fundamentally telepathic—the induction of hallucination of a change in shape—and not an actual psychokinetic rearrangement of matter. More will be said of this in the next chapter on mediumship itself. Needless to say, these kinds of telepathically induced hallucinations, while psychic in nature, are not truly *clairvoyant*.

Regarding seeing at a distance, there are multiple approaches that can be taken here. Using tendrils as before, as if we were contacting a spirit at a distance, we can reach into a location and feel around the fields in the room. From the different feelings in the room, we can begin to get an idea of what is in there, and with some time we may even be able to resolve spatial locations. However, because this effect depends on our recognition of the energetic reflections of physical objects (or spirits, as the case may be), it's important to note that the clairvoyant using this method will have a difficult time naming objects with which he or she is not familiar. Physical properties are not being communicated, and a person who has never seen, for example, a windmill turbine, will not be able to recognize it from its energy. Instead, he or she may come up with other descriptions that are disorganized and unmapped.

Readers may be familiar with the practice of *remote viewing*, which is somewhat related to clairvoyance. In remote viewing the viewer gathers information about a remote site psychically while adhering to a strict protocol that both enables the viewing task and removes risk of spoiling interference. In remote viewing, it is critical that the viewer not be aware of what the site is and not be too familiar with the site; familiarity with the site can lead to "analytical overlay," which is not unlike the problems we discussed previously regarding telepathy. Essentially, as soon as the viewer begins to guess or imagine what the target is through analysis of the information, they will no longer be receptive to psychic information about the remote site. Contrary to this approach, the clairvoyant actually needs to be familiar with the site. Not in the sense that he or she knows what the site location is (in that case it's likely he or she would just imagine it, which is not a psychic exercise!), but in the sense that he or she is familiar with things available in the site.

The process here is that the energy is impressing onto the field, and then the mind is forming a perception based on recognition and familiarity. In the previous case of a windmill turbine, it's possible that a clairvoyant might report a plane propeller. This is because those properties are present in both, and the mind does not know what the actual thing is, and so substitutes the next closest match. Similarly, when clairvoyantly viewing a castle, it's possible the mind will fill in *a castle*, but not necessarily *the* castle that is being viewed. The component pieces are there and the image is being identified via *bottom-up processing*, but the finer details may not be there at all. The world of the psychic is abstract, not concrete, and the more quickly we become comfortable with this ambiguity and instability, the more successful we will be. We might be able to identify a bedroom, and where the bed is or was, but the style of bed is perhaps a degree of accuracy too far. It's important to focus on details that advance our understanding of the narrative, the story, *what happened*, and not quibble about inconsequential and unimportant details. A fixation on accurate details without a comprehensible narrative is only useful if our aim is to demonstrate the reality of our claims, and this is not in and of itself a useful thing to do. While training, picking out individual details can be very exciting and can be a tremendous boost for our confidence, but fixating on it too much can lead to a toxic mindset that inhibits our actual learning.

Clairvoyance via Gazing

The second approach to clairvoyance is one that relies on a tool or device for the spirit to appear in, called a *speculum*. The speculum, then, can be any substrate that allows for appearances to arise while we are focused on it. Perhaps the most stereotypical speculum is the crystal ball, but elaborate specula like this are not necessary by any means. A black matte circle on a white card, a dark colored bowl filled with water, and a dark or silver mirror are all examples of effective specula which can be commonly obtained. There is nothing magical about the device itself. Rather, it is a medium into which we look to allow information to manifest. The dark coloration is intended not to fatigue the eyes and to incline us into trance. We *lean in* mentally, allowing ourselves to be consumed in our focus on the speculum, and whatever arises we note accordingly. The images that arise can be of many sorts. Rarely, we can get an actual image of the spirit or the location or the information that we're seeking, presented plainly. More commonly, the information will be of a deeply symbolic nature. Here we return to the inner work discussed earlier, and the importance of knowing what symbols mean to us. It may happen that we see flowers, for example, or parting clouds, and this may have absolutely nothing to do with the actual target. Instead, flowers may represent harmony for us, and parting clouds a sense of relief. These kinds of symbols are internal to ourselves. There is no universal symbolic language, each person recognizes these symbols for themselves, and it is an error to believe that a color or image would have a universal meaning.

When trying to work with spirits, we may see the spirit itself or its message being communicated through the speculum. This, too, may arrive symbolically. The spirit may try to relay its own symbols, but it should be emphasized that the spirit should try to use the concepts themselves which it means to communicate. Generally, in both cases the thing that appears to the clairvoyant will be in his or her own symbolic language, but in the case that it is not the spirit should be gently encouraged to use concepts that work, or to "decode" the information telepathically.

The actual process of clairvoyance using specula is very straightforward, as we have already established the preliminaries in practicing meditation and noticing. Before, we rested the mind on an arbitrary object and simply brought the mind back to it. Now, we should rest the mind on the speculum and observe for subtle signs or changes in our visual field. It can help to have a variable light such as a candle, but usually it is better for it to be mostly dark. The light can play tricks on its own, and so may interfere with clean communication. On the other hand, some spirits prefer to manipulate the light to cast images onto the speculum. For the most part, this is uncommon. The images in the speculum arise to us, in our own mind, as if being projected. This information is being obtained through the subconscious and its interactions with the world, and the speculum provides a screen upon which the images can be case by the unconscious mind in order to communicate them to the conscious mind. Thus, there is no need for artificial physical means to project images onto the speculum, as the images that will appear will appear to us as if being played there by projection. While candlelight or other kinds of moving, dynamic light can add ambience and incline us towards the appropriate trance, their presence is not necessary for the formation of images because the images themselves arise only within our minds.

For the same reason, there is no need to attempt to record or photograph the visions that arise within the speculum. Whatever visions should be documented in a thorough manner so they can be reviewed later, because it will be impossible to view them again. The clairvoyant may choose to take notes by hand during the clairvoyant trance, to report visions out loud while recording audio, or to have an associate function as a handler or operator who is responsible for recording notes and observations and debriefing the clairvoyant.

Consistency here is key. Clairvoyance is a fickle enough process as it stands, prone to error or a lack of information and deeply steeped in symbolic language. If we are not consistent in how we apply the techniques, it will be impossible to accurately judge what gives us good results versus bad results, and this leaves our results up to chance rather than skill development. Only by consistently working and only changing small variables at a time can we improve our technique. And, as W.E. Butler has noted in *How to Read the Aura,* clairvoyance is more of an art than an exact science. There is no exact technique that, if followed, will result in perfectly clear information. As much of the skill comes in interpreting inner symbolism and understanding the ways in which psychic information presents itself as comes from actually being receptive to the psychic information in the first place. Limiting the variation between sessions helps to limit other factors so that we know what to focus on when we "miss."

Mediumship and Channeling

Broadly speaking, much of the last few chapters has been about mediumship. Whenever a spirit communicates through a person, that person is functioning as a medium. Whether they are telepathically receiving information from the spirit that they repackage into a new format, or they are clairvoyantly seeing images a spirit intends to communicate, a person who serves as the method of communication for a spirit is nothing other than a medium. However, often this term is reserved for a venerable tradition of individuals who exclusively communicate on behalf of spirits. Often these people will have one or just a few controls, and they will operate from a trance state. Classic examples of trance mediums include Allan Kardec, the founder of Spiritism, and Edgar Cayce, an American mystic who channeled medical advice and diagnoses. These also represent different approaches to mediumship: whereas Kardec channeled any number of spirits, Cayce seems to have worked with only a few controls. A *control* is the spirit that is operating the *medium* for purposes of communication.

In paranormal investigation, it is more common for a medium to be communicating for the local spirits directly than via a familiar control, though admittedly it is entirely possible for a medium with a recurring to control to have that control act as a proxy. That is, some mediums will have their regular control speak to other spirits, then they will channel the control, who reports on the discussion. It is also less common for paranormal investigation teams to employ trance mediums, as trance mediums typically need more specific circumstances to be effective, and because trance mediums are by definition not "themselves" during their trance, so they cannot really be relied upon to be giving accurate impressions. A trance medium's recollections of events may be spotty and inconsistent, so they can only give limited feedback later on about their state and observations. However, for workings involving spirits, a trance medium may have a much easier time of establishing a direct line of communication, and invocation is a very traditional approach to working with spirits.

Perhaps the biggest difference between a medium who uses telepathy, empathy, clairvoyance, or so further to communicate with a spirit and the trance medium is the degree of control surrendered to the spirit. In telepathy, the spirit and the psychic remain distinct and communicate much as two people standing in a room together. However, the trance medium often instead relies on *channeling*, and this usually refers to the spirit speaking directly through the medium. Instead of the medium receiving a communication then relaying it either in the voice of an interpreter or in the voice of a reporter, the spirit assumes control of the body of the medium and so directly speaks. The medium is truly only a vehicle by which the spirit communicates, in this use, hence the term.

Channeling carries a significantly greater number of risks versus other kinds of communication with and by spirits. Obvious risks include that the spirit may not yield back control of a physical body it is borrowing, at which case the channeling becomes a "possession." In some cases, the channeling is narrow in scope, and so becomes something like automatic writing, discussed in a later section. Even here, a spirit can become unwilling to return control of the body to the medium. Another risk is that of addiction. For many mediums, the opportunity to cede control of the body to another can be an enjoyable, pleasant feeling. Stepping out of control of one's body tends to accompany a release from feelings of stress and obligation. The surrender to the spirit is something like a vacation away from the body, and trance states, which can range from very light to extremely deep, are generally very pleasant once one has recognized and surrendered to the loss of control.

It is this surrender that is the most difficult part of trance mediumship or channeling. Trances in general require some degree of surrender. Most trance states result in dampened or slowed physical reactions to the environment, or in some cases a complete dissociation from the physical body altogether. These states leave a person vulnerable, and not being in control of the body means being quite literally out of control of one's actions. When this kind of trance occurs involuntarily, it is very often traumatic, as can be the case in certain types of possession, or when someone has been drugged without his or her knowledge. However, once such a feeling is surrendered into, there is an immediate state of catharsis and release. This is not unlike skydiving, SCUBA diving, or riding on a rollercoaster. Once we surrender to the experience, it can be enjoyable to let whatever happens happen, but until we achieve that state of resignation, the experience can be terrifying.

In short, whether or not one will make a good trance medium depends entirely on a few psychological factors, including hypnotic susceptibility (the ability to be hypnotized) and the ability to surrender to an experience. These may in fact be reflections of the same underlying psychological trait, as those who are unable to surrender and release control of themselves also tend to be more resistant to hypnosis. While it's not necessarily true that a person must be *willing* in order to be hypnotized, it is certainly true that there are some people who cannot be hypnotized and that an unwillingness to be hypnotized as well as the psychological wherewithal to recognize and resist hypnotic attempts makes for a powerful protective factor. This same protective factor applies to the trance medium, and attempts to resist a trance are very likely to be affective for those individuals. Others, who more readily submit to hypnosis, are far more likely to be able to drop into a trance sufficient for mediumship.

All mediums essentially have their own way of both reaching trance and allowing the spirit to take over, generally through intentional invitation. Because trance mediumship is at its core passive, allowing the spirit to take over, it can be difficult to describe techniques or methods. The ability to relax and allow oneself into a trance state is the primary skill involved, with the most difficult part being surrendering control and stepping aside to allow the spirit to take control. Spirits like the Tibetan Dorje Drakpo will assume control of the medium's body and dance around with it in ritual movements, before pronouncing their prophecy in archaic Tibetan language. Other spirits who take ritual possession of people involve the Loa of the voodoo traditions. Both of these take place from within a context of ritual invocation. Trance mediums can have very active sessions like these, but more commonly the spirit assumes control of the body only to speak and sometimes gesture. I suspect that speech is fairly automatic, whereas a spirit may not know how the finer details of controlling a physical human body. In any case, a more common trance medium setting will be laying on the back with the eyes closed and the hands folded in the lap, as was the method of Edgar Cayce.

To actually conduct the session, each trance medium will have her or her own specific technique here as well. A new medium who is working primarily off of information learned from this book should first establish telepathic contact with the spirit. After this contact is established, the medium can invite the spirit into the body and enter the trance state. Entering a trance state is an auto-hypnotic practice that can be similar, but is not strictly related, to meditation. If the medium has previously been hypnotized, this should be fairly familiar.

A very simple self-hypnosis routine resembles other hypnotic routines fairly closely. Begin by relaxing, finding a place to sit comfortably or lay down with an object to focus the eyes on. Take deep breaths and relax your muscles progressively. Start by tensing the toes and tense then relax each muscle in turn up the body until the shoulders, and then down to the tips of the fingers. Take deep, slow breathes making sure to exhale completely. While staying focused on the object, begin to count backwards from ten, reciting each time "I am relaxing." Allow the eyes to feel heavy and close on their own. As you progress deeper into the hypnotic state, tell yourself that when you reach "one" you will be in a full trance. You may accompany this with a visualization, such as walking down a flight of stairs and visualizing each floor as a number. When you read the first floor, you are fully entranced. All of this serves to get us into a hypnotic state where we can allow the spirit to take control of our body to speak through it. You may visualize yourself leaving the "control room" of your body and allowing the spirit to be seated there, using your own inner symbolism. When the session should end, you can visualize yourself going back up the stairs, or back into the "control room." Your monitor should know how to bring you out of a hypnotic trance if necessary, though generally the worst case scenario from the hypnosis itself is just that you will fall asleep and wake up naturally.

Despite that there's not much to be said regarding the medium except those skills typically associated with being a good hypnotic subject, there is a great deal more to say for those who would serve as handlers for a trance medium. The trance medium always depends on another party both for his or her own safety as well as to document the events of the trance and to direct questions to the control. Because the medium is by definition out of control of his or her own body, he or she can neither be relied upon to direct questions or to recall any of the session. Many trance mediums will have very little recollection, if any at all, of the session. Others will have a very vague recollection, like in a dream. Regardless, the trance medium is not reliable for providing any information about the session itself, except in cases like automatic writing, discussed later.

It is not sufficient to simply set a camera or recording, as the spirit will not have anyone to prompt questions. Even when these questions are planned in advance, they cannot be reliably communicated by the medium. And it is entirely possible that the camera could malfunction either through the influence of spirits or just by following Murphy's Law. If the information is important enough to warrant a trance medium to find, it's important enough to rate proper recording, and so trance mediumship is at least a two person operation.

The handler's responsibility are, as mentioned, threefold: first, the handler must ensure the safety of the medium. Next, the handler is responsible for interacting with the spirit, asking questions as determined in advance of the session. Finally, the handler (or yet another assistant, the stenographer) is responsible for recording whatever answers come.

These second two roles do not require much extrapolation. The role of the stenographer is quite obvious. The stenographer needs simply record a transcript of the session, including the words of all present. This can be done through a video or audio recording, as well as by hand. It is generally good practice to have multiple redundant recording devices. Electronic devices can and do malfunction during séance activity, including trance mediumship. A physical, written copy can also reveal discrepancies between perception and actuality, which sometimes happens when a spirit is communicating through a person. If manual transcripts are being made, this almost always should be another person entirely. The handler should be singularly focused on performing his or her responsibilities according to the preferences of the medium. Manually transcribing notes while also talking to a spirit is no easy task, and it's very likely to introduce mistakes into the record if not into the session itself.

Directing the questions to the spirit is a slightly more involved task. The questions should be prepared in advance, and pre-planned. Generally, it's best to ask only those things that have been agreed upon. These questions should *not* be shared with the medium. It is never appropriate to inform a medium about the questions in advance if only because this can lead to the difficulties in surrendering to the spirit without loading in one's own imagined responses. It should not need to be explained that this can also lead to concerns about fraud and deception. Self-deception is by far the worst form for the medium, and giving those questions in advance can lead to a particularly imaginative medium deluding him or herself into foolishness. But the questions *should* be agreed upon, generally between the handler and any others involved in the investigation, or with the person asking the questions in the event of a divination for another sitter. This is *not* necessarily the case in the parlor séance with a trance medium who is channeling for spirits in the room. In that case, the various sitters can each ask their own questions; though it's generally best that they have planned these in advance.

Even in these group settings, however, there must be a single individual responsible for fulfilling the role of a handler. It is important that a single individual be control of a session should things go wrong. Ideally, this individual should be familiar with the material in this book and able to conduct an exorcism of some sort, though this isn't strictly necessary. This person should also have a good rapport with the trance medium, though this does not necessarily have to be a long or close connection, but there can be problems when the medium and handler are not on good terms. Much of the medium's safety is in the hands of the handler, and so there must at least be mutual trust. The handler has considerable power over the medium, as the medium is absent in the trance state and will not have clear recollection necessarily. Thus the two must be able to trust one another.

Safety for the medium does not mean only during the trance state itself. The handler must also assume responsibility to care for the medium in the hours following a trance. Many mediums will be extremely tired and sometimes somewhat delirious upon the spirit's departure. The transition can be jarring and the act of channeling is exhausting in its own right. Some mediums sleep immediately after the spirit departs, some awaken but are uncoordinated and disoriented. The handler should be familiar with the medium's needs for care and provide for his or her safety and comfort. Additionally, the handler generally assumes responsibility for arranging the setting and making sure the medium has what he or she needs. Most trance mediums are aware of their needs as well as what they need after the session, and can, if necessary, teach someone to act as a handler in advance.

Automatic Writing

A subset of channeling is *automatic writing*. Automatic writing is a practice of receiving written messages through spirits, where the medium is either in a trance or otherwise not in control of the writing. This may or may not involve the same kind of possession as mediumship or channeling. Sometimes, it is just the spirit guiding the hand directly. It requires a bit less surrender than normal channeling, as the spirit is only given control over the hand for the purpose of writing. It is still a powerful tool for channeling as it allows the spirit to communicate full, long-form messages.

The practice is relatively simple and straightforward, but does take some preparatory work on the part of the medium. It's difficult to allow our hand to move independently of our conscious control, and this is the part that takes practice. Just as the trance medium needs to be able to step aside and relax conscious control of the body, the automatic writer must be able to allow the hand to move independently without consciously interjecting on the motion. It's also important that the writer be able to separate his or her attention from the process. Analysis of what is being written can lead to attempting to "guess" the message, which corrupts the process just as with other forms of channeling.

Learning to release control can be done through practicing free writing. Free writing is a technique used by writers to prepare to write, where one writes freely without regard to grammar, spelling, form, or content. What is important is that the pen is moving uninhibited. When used as a prewriting practice it is meant to start ideas and to engage the mind to the task of writing. Here, we are using it as a way of practicing the uninhibited movement of the hand in the writing process. The goal is to remove the analytical mind from the process of writing. If we can free write successfully, we have accomplished the first step; the hand is moving without our analytical mind starting it only when there is meaningful content and stopping it when we don't know the next thing coming.

Once we have achieved this, we can begin the work in much the same way as we already have. The automatic writer can invite the spirit and enter into a trance, though this trance is not necessarily as deep or complete as those used by other kinds of channels. The automatic writer should not be looking at the paper; whether this is accomplished by blindfolding, closed eyes, or a screen between the medium's hand and face. The purpose for this is to further ensure that the medium not censor the content, not to attempt to maintain any kind of parapsychological scientific rigor or prove the effect is authentic. It's quite obvious that a fraudulent medium could produce automatic writing regardless of a blindfold or screen, so the purpose of this should not be mistaken. It is purely a convention of assisting the medium in not analyzing and influencing the information manually, and not an attempt at adding legitimacy.

Another form of automatic writing involves the planchette, or "little plank," a small piece of wood in which a pen can be inserted. The movements of the planchette through the guidance of a spirit spells out a message. This removes the medium's direct influence over the process by a degree, as most of us can write by hand, but writing by moving a planchette is an unfamiliar task. The spirit is able to direct our movement-impulse by exerting telepathic influence on our unconscious mind, and it is not necessary for the message to rise to the conscious mind. However, it is much easier to remove our conscious mind from the process of guiding a planchette than to remove our conscious mind's influence from a usually conscious activity like writing. Thus this form of automatic writing is often easier to achieve success with, though the message usually must be much shorter, both due to the time it takes to spell out the message and due to the physical and mental fatigue that comes from the process.

Talking Boards

Another form of automatic writing is the talking board, which first became popular in the West in the late 1800s, particularly among spiritualists. In 1890, Elijah Bond patented the talking board in association with Charles Kennard of the Kennard Novelty Company. Kennard named it the "Ouija board," and a number of apocryphal stories exist as to where this name comes from. According to Kennard, the name was derived in a session with the board. Sitting with medium Helen Peters Nosworthy, they determined to ask what to name the board, and it spelled out "OUIJA." When they asked what it meant, they were told "Good Luck." In the early 1900s, William Fuld obtained the rights to the "Ouija" name, and despite a number of competitor products, most people now know talking boards by the Ouija brand name.

Talking boards differ from automatic writing in a number of ways. The most obvious is the method of operation.

As discussed previously, automatic writing generally involves either a medium entering into a light trance with the spirit directing a freewriting activity, or a medium allowing the spirit to guide his or her hand in directing a planchette which writes directly onto a paper. The talking board, by contrast, has the letters arranged in advance, and the spirit directs the planchette around the options via the operator.

Another difference, and one of the major reasons for their popularity among spiritualists in the 1800s and the public today, is that one does not have to be a medium to operate a talking board. Whereas most automatic writing requires some preparation and training, and the ability to contact and invite spirits to use one as a medium, the talking board allows spirits a means to communicate without a skilled psychic operator. Again there is the exception of planchette-based automatic writing systems here, where the same kinds of motions and effects result in a message. However, planchette writing still requires significant skill and, importantly in the late 1800s, the ability to write. While literacy was on the rise during the industrial revolution, it was still far from a universal skill. While it's certainly more impressive and verifiably psychic for an illiterate person to perform automatic writing, it's also a far less accessible skill. Just as the autoharp made music accessible in the parlor of families in the late 19th century, the talking board made mediumship available to common people.

Some believe that the talking board does not involve spirits at all, but instead allows for the transference of information from the latent psychic perceptions of the operators. In some cases this may well be true. A psychic who has not learned to recognize intuition may use a talking board or the like to transmit information. Because of the way a talking board works, his or her unconscious influence will guide the planchette to provide his or her own answers to questions. The same can be said for pendulum dowsing, discussed later in this book.

A talking board does not have to be an expensive hardwood board or a cardboard game board from Hasbro. The fundamentals are fairly simple: the alphabet is arranged on a board or piece of paper, and a planchette is moved along the surface of the board to point to letters. The spirit is asked questions and through subtle influence guides the participants' hands to steer the planchette, thus spelling out the answers. Generally at least two operators are involved, keeping their fingers lightly touching the planchette. It should be allowed to glide smoothly and evenly, and sudden feelings of resistance, scraping, or hard pushing often indicate someone is trying to "force" the planchette.

Because the whole operation is steered largely by the ideomotor effect and by individuals each responding unconsciously to one another's subtle pushes, it is possible for the reading to happen without any spirit present at all. Indeed, critics of the use of talking boards claim that this means *all* such uses are guided purely in this way. But I know of no one who claims the planchette is being operated through a spirit's psychokinetic influence. Instead, the spirit is influencing the minds of the operators, sending a message to the unconscious. The planchette's movement through ideomotor effect is a mechanism by which the unconscious message is brought to conscious awareness. Whether or not a particular talking board session is truly involving spirits has to be determined by the information gained and other factors.

There are a great number of different designs of boards; there's nothing magical or special about the layout of the board that makes them work. Today, the most common arrangement by far is alphabetical, in two rows of 13 letters each, with numbers one through zero in their own row (or two) and commonly with "yes," "no," "hello," and "goodbye" as well.

Figure 1 - Kennard-Bond Ouija board, Baltimore, MD, ca. 1890. Photo courtesy of the Museum of Talking Boards.

An example of this design is seen in Figure 1[10]. This design dates to 1890, but is likely familiar; the basic design has remained unchanged for over a hundred years.

Despite the popularity of this arrangement, any configuration of the alphabet and numerals works. Iconography on commercial boards is generally just marketing, and not an important part of the board's function. For example, the sun and moon are found in the corners of the "Good Night" board in Figure 1, but these were common decorations at the time. Similarly, the "yes," no," and so on are not strictly necessary; these are merely shortcuts for making those kinds of questions simpler.

---

[10] This photo as well as the other talking board photos are provided with the generous permission of the Museum of Talking Boards. A wealth of information for those interested in talking boards can be found at their home on the web, located at https:// museumoftalkingboards.com/ at time of writing.

In fact, the arrangement is far from universal. Many older boards used more rows, for example. There is an argument to be made for the other designs, as well. For example, an alphabetical arrangement makes sense to us as operators, and so if the unconscious instruction is "push to J," we can generally gauge where "J" is from the current planchette position. On the other hand, if our goal is something verifiably psychic, our foreknowledge of where the letters are arranged does little to mitigate the accusation of a fraudulent medium "forcing" the message, regardless of how many operators are involved. Some boards use an arbitrary arrangement of the alphabet as a result, as this reduces the likelihood of "forcing" the message, especially when everyone involved is unfamiliar with the board arrangement.

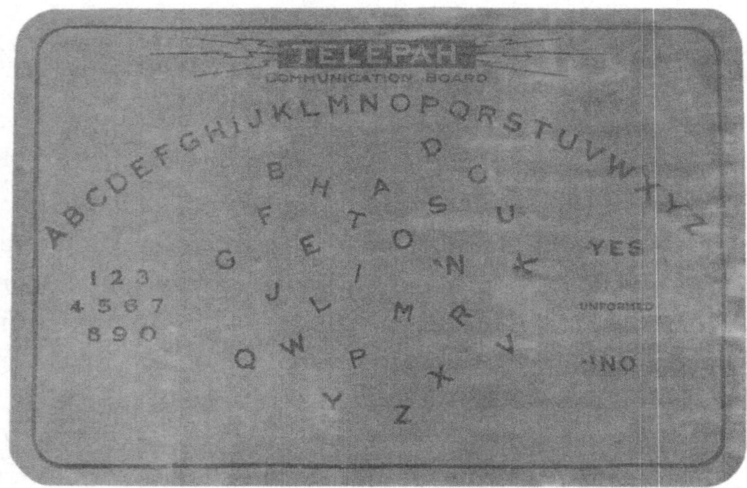

Figure 2 - A "Telepah" Board, designed for the Psychic Research Association in Salem, MA, ca. 1919. Photo courtesy the Museum of Talking Boards.

The "Telepah" board in Figure 2 is an example of this concept, featuring both an arbitrary assemblage of letters in the center as well as a single row alphabetical arrangement. While the unconscious mind should still be able to operate the planchette successfully, the hypothesis goes, the conscious mind would struggle to form words or sentences with an arbitrary arrangement of letters. Of course, this is no real assurance against fraud. As always, it's best to simply associate with

Figure 3 - Reed "Espirito" board, Leominster, MA ca. 1891. Courtesy of the Museum of Talking Boards.

known good faith actors and not concern ourselves with fraud.

The problem of needing to cover significant distance to reach common letters is also mitigated by using an arrangement of letters with more rows. This is not a modern innovation, but rather dates back to the earliest boards. It is largely a function of the branding and the vast number of imitations and variations on the original designs that as resulted in the two-row convention. In some cases, time-saving phrases or even grammatical structures are included in addition to letters and numbers. These save considerable time, as the messages don't need to be spread out. This is already common practice for "yes," "no," and "goodbye" on the standard Ouija board.

There are as many designs of planchettes as there are boards. Most are large enough that multiple people can get at least one or two fingers of each hands on it, while being small enough to still be operated by a single person using one or both hands. A vaguely arrowhead or heart shape is most common, though there are many others. Most differences are more in the interest of brand identity than functionality, however. Any shape with a pointer or indicator that allows us to see clearly the letter being communicated will work.

Planchettes for automatic writing generally had a hole to insert a writing tool upright. This is reflected in many modern designs as well. In the early 1900s it became common for the planchette to have a viewing window rather in the place where a pen holder would go. Whether one uses a viewing window or the pointer to indicate letters is a matter of personal preference, and if the planchette has a viewing window an interesting exercise is to note the letter indicated by both the arrow and the viewing window until a message begins to become clear.

The planchette should be smooth and able to slide across the surface with little resistance. Some planchettes rest on top of ball bearings to allow them to roll smoothly with very little resistance. Planchettes used for writing (or based on them) will have sometimes have caster wheels on two sides with the pen mounted in the middle. Some very cheap planchettes sit directly on the smooth surface of the board, but this design requires a high degree of polish on both board and planchette to work. The most common today tend to be plastic planchettes with three "legs," sometimes one of them in the middle of the viewing window. This strikes a good compromise between stability and resistance.

Operation of the talking board can be with one, two, or even more individuals. It is not strictly necessary to have two operators, though it can help to prevent our own preconceptions or ideas from driving the session. If more than one person is using the board, it should be placed between them an equal distance. Unequal placement provides one or the other with a mechanical advantage that somewhat defeats the purpose of having two operators in the first place. The stereotypical placement is resting in the lap or on the legs of both operators, seated on the floor, but this is again by no means necessary. Simply placing it on a table is enough.

In session, a question should be stated aloud and held in mind. The operator should not have to provide any conscious direction to the planchette, neither pushing nor pulling. Instead, the hands should simply be allowed to guide the planchette in its movement, stopping when it feels right to stop. If there are two operators, this feeling can be a little clearer, because the other person will continue pushing. The mutual push and pull leads to a kind of consensus on the message. Optionally, a third person, not involved in the exercise, can record each letter. Ideally, the operators should not remove their hands from the planchette when a message is incoming, but should instead stay focused on the question, paying attention to the pressures and feelings in the hand.

While anyone *can* operate a talking board, it is a skill like any other. It is not necessary to enter a non-volitional trance to allow a spirit to inhabit the body and "take control" as in channeling, or even to relinquish the control of a limb to a spirit as in automatic writing, but interpreting the inputs of the spirit still requires practice and experience. The best way, of course, is to work with the board, taking notes on differences between successes and failures.

Offering and Purifying

In addition to the strictly psychic approaches, there are approaches from more traditional folk magic that can help us substantially. I've referred to spirits having likes and dislikes. Of course, we can charge a field or room with properties they dislike, but this requires a large amount of skill. In fact, much of the psychic material in this book requires lots of time and practice. We may need to do something more immediate that does not require so much preparatory work. Fortunately, there are more mechanistic methods to driving off or summoning spirits using materials they like or dislike. We can offer spirits things that they like, including homes where they can stay, and in this way we can bring them to a place or contain them to an area. Alternatively, we can fill an area with things spirits dislike, and so force them out or drive them away.

Offerings

In India, deities receive traditional offerings that mirror what would be given to a king in procession or guest in the home. These deities are offered water for washing the face, water for drinking, perfumed water for cleaning the body, food, lights, incense, and music. Some spirits will also be offered a cup of tea or alcohol. These are symbolic offerings usually arranged in bowls on the altar, but the displays can be much more elaborate. Across the world, Vodou practitioners offer Papa Legba rum and cigars. Christians make offerings of money, time and effort in the form of prayers, recitations, and masses, candles, and incense. In the ancient world, the slaughter of animals was common as offerings to the gods.

Local spirits tend not to require so much. Most of us are not dealing with gods, though we may be dealing with powerful regional guardians or protectors. Many spirits will let us know what they like for offerings, but before that can happen we have to have their attention and presence. For most, we can think about their natures. Candles are a good selection, and also serve as a medium. Clean water or tea works well. Food is always a good option, though it is best to stick to grain products. Some spirits do not care for meats, some do. Some spirits will react angrily towards certain vegetables or fruits. Many will simply not be interested at all. Grain offerings are generally neutral or inoffensive.

I usually start with whiskey and cookies. If these are offerings to sacred beings that we intend to worship or respect, we should make sure it's fresh. We should open a new bottle and bake new cookies or open a fresh box. For most spirits, I don't think it's necessary to have new things. It *is* important that it not be spoiled. Offering stale food to a houseguest would be considered a slight. It's no different with spirits. Whiskey and cookies are usually accepted by most spirits, however. Adding some water or milk to the mix can bring it to completion. A fruit on the plate wouldn't hurt to round it out. Consider it like setting a spread for a guest.

When making the offering, there is no need for an elaborate ritual. It can help if you're conducting a parlor séance or something like this. Generally, placing them out and designating the space is sufficient. A table or mantle or wherever we want the spirit to manifest is the right place. If we're conducting a paranormal investigation we should set the offerings where our recording and measurement equipment is found. If we're conducting a séance, a table in front of the medium is a good option. In the séance setting, you might consider setting a plate for the spirits, placing snacks on the plate, then sharing in the meal by enjoying snacks prior to beginning the séance proper. It's worth remembering that parlor séances were generally social events, in the form of small parties. Often, the medium was as much entertainment as conduit to the world beyond. The light and cheerful atmosphere was meant to attract the spirits of the deceased to their loved ones. Today many séances conducted outside the Spiritualist community have taken on a serious and somber tone. We have other forms of entertainment for idle diversions, so we take the séance very seriously. It's little surprise, then, that we either get serious spirits or practical jokers.

Spirits of locations will often enjoy things that can be inferred by the qualities of their locations. Nature spirits appreciate the bounties of nature, but not reminders of our exploitation of nature. Fresh fruits and flowers are good, dried foods or cut flowers are not so good. Fire can be a reminder of devastation and destruction, and may seem like more of a threat than an offering. Water can be a good offering, as it brings life. Water is not a good offering to fire spirits, obviously. It can be an acceptable offering to those that live in water, but not always so. After all, spirits who live in water have plenty of water, and offering some more may not accomplish anything, especially if it's contained in a bottle or bowl. Why move into a bowl when one has a pond? Fire elementals of course refer fire or ash, dry wood, and so further. When working with elementals, the placement of offerings is best done where those elementals already are likely to be found: fire in fireplaces and chimneys, water in sinks or tubs, earth in basements and cellars, air in attics and on high balconies.

The purpose of these offerings is straightforward: we are asking the spirits politely to come, rather than trying to badger or harass them into responding to us. This is certainly a better approach when a medium intends to channel the spirit. It's also a good approach if we just seek information through divination techniques.

It is best to leave offerings in place for at least 24 hours, to allow the spirits a chance to consume their spiritual essence. Afterwards they should be disposed of where people do not walk, and not in the trash. Offerings to spirits one wishes to leave should be offered inside but then immediately taken outside to the property boundary, or ideally further, to a crossroad. It is sometimes believed that spirits cannot find their way back from a crossroads. Others might suggest that spirits brought to a crossroad will be helped along by crossroad spirits to find new grounds. Whatever the reason, a crossroad is a powerful place to lead an unwanted spirit. Offerings to land spirits can be offered inside and then disposed of outside if we want the spirit to appear inside. Otherwise they can be offered at the location. It is best to dispose of offerings of alcohol, tea, water, and so on by pouring it directly onto the soil, again, in a place where people do not walk. Offerings of food should be put somewhere where animals can get to it. This allows spirits with preferred animals to manifest or call them to eat the offerings, and it serves as a continued act of generosity, so that the offering's intended purpose is not changed. Because a spirit puts some of itself in the offering when it's accepted, it is best not to throw anything out once it's been offered, as this can be seen as a slight.

Cleansing

We may need to clean ourselves or clean a house and may not have the skill to do so by manipulation of psychic energy alone. How we do so depends again on the type of influence we are trying to clean away. We don't usually want to experiment with these materials, unless we have significant experience working with herbs and understand it at a deeper level. It's possible to cause ourselves a lot of harm by working with plants we're unfamiliar with or using plants without recognizing their effects.

Cleansing areas is usually done through the use of incense, smudges, and washes.

Incense is burned and the smoke allowed to travel around the room naturally. The type of incense matters, and there are many different incenses for many different purposes.

For the purpose of cleansing, juniper is a strong contender. This incense purifies negativity and drives off negative spirits. You don't want to be stingy with an incense when using it alone, and you don't really want to pair this incense with other offering incenses. Sometimes this practice is referred to as *smudging*, though the backgrounds are slightly different. When smudging, the plant is generally still whole. Rather than ground into a powder, it is bundled into a stick and dried. It is then burned with a coal, rather than lit directly. The exact mechanism doesn't matter so much as the smoke and that it is produced naturally. Other purifying incenses include frankincense and white sage.

Washes are used for cleaning and preparing floors magically. The usual process is the same as mopping, though using herbs that encourage desirable energies. This can be used to either attract spirits or repel them based on the spirits' preferences. Common ingredients in floor washes include peppermint, rosemary, rue, and lavender. This incorporates protective properties with cleansing properties and wards against the evil eye. The preparation is simple: boil the dried or fresh leaves of the ingredients for a few minutes to create a tea-like elixir. Strain the solids, and mix the concoction with pure water. Then mop the floor with it, taking care to move from the inside areas of each room to the outside, from back to front and left to right. It is especially important to attend to corners and energetic "eddies" that prevent the flow of energy through the room. Once the mopping is complete, allow it to dry in the air. Obviously don't do this in rooms with carpet, and take care with hardwood floors. Today, most people use smudges and incense exclusively. However, the full wash can be extraordinarily effective as it suffuses the entire room with the essences of the herbs used. It is important that one uses herbs that have been established to "work together," taking special care not to mix herbs that are not known to work together, as they can cancel one another out or create strange reactions that can attract negativity.

Baths are also used to purifying oneself. After traveling into haunted homes with strong negative presences or especially after driving an unwanted spirit from a home, it is important that we protect ourselves. The exorcist in particular must be sure to clean and purify afterwards, as a displaced spirit is often looking for a new haunt, and may be unhappy with the exorcist. In addition to grounding and centering, bathing with peppermint, rue, and baking soda can help purify one's energetic field and prevent one from being followed easily. A general-use cleansing bath to avert the evil eye and to drive off negative spirits is a beer bath. Adding a bottle of beer to a tub of warm water, mix in a tablespoon of salt, and stir until it is mixed evenly. Then bathe for at least 10 minutes, making sure to completely wash the entire body, pouring water over oneself with a cup and scrubbing thoroughly. Afterwards, allow yourself to air dry off. It is usually best to do this before bed, and not before important business meetings or driving, in case the odor of beer causes you problems (though it will not be too strong). The type of beer does matter, and American beers made with rice or high fructose corn syrup should be avoided. Instead, traditional lagers or dark beers are better.

Another useful technique for diverting spirits is the use of *witch bottles*. A witch bottle is a bottle used to attract spirits that are attracted to us. It is filled with material sympathetic to us: nail clippings, hair, and urine are good examples. Often, it is also filled with iron nails, barbed wire, and razors. It is then sealed and buried outside a fair distance from where we live. Because spirits often navigate by our energetic signature, they can be lured to the bottle and trapped within by the iron. Spirits that are looking to follow us may become distracted and end up there. This also works as a defense against sorcery if the sorcerer does not have a clear sympathetic link to us.

Divination

Divination generally refers to any kind of supernatural or preternatural technique for finding information about the past, present, or future that otherwise would not be accessible. Looking in an almanac or checking the weather channel is not divination, counting crows or poking holes in the ground might. Sometimes an almanac may be composed of information that has been divined, especially older almanacs, but most of the time they are composed through statistical analysis. Most divinatory techniques rely on the diviner operating some kind device or method to gain insight; for example, interpreting Tarot cards or astrological charting. We've already covered one form of divination in the section on talking boards, which can be used for divination without spirits just as easily as with spirits. Other techniques exist, however. The method we use is largely a function of the form of answer we want.

When we use these methods of divination with a spirit, it's important to consider what the spirit might know. A local protector spirit probably won't have access to information about events in other countries. A land guardian probably won't have much information about things in the future that don't have to do with its land. Both will likely have information about the persons or places they protect in the present and the past. They may have information about threats or dangers, obstacles, obstructions, or the motivations or activities of other spirits nearby. They may have information about people who live or have lived in a place. It's always worth asking "do you know anything about . . . " before broaching a subject, as spirits may save you a lot of time by simply answering "no."

Notice that these divinatory techniques assume cooperation. This is not an interrogation or an attempt to coerce information out of the spirit. We're asking the spirit's cooperation on the basis of friendship, or at least not hostility.

While techniques *do* exist for coercing spirits using interrogation, these are not consistent with the methods of this book. It is better to foster cooperative relationships rather than dominance and power games. If a spirit is hostile or uncooperative, it may refuse to answer, or it may engage in deception. Both of these are possible even if they do intend to cooperate, but far less likely depending on the questions and your reasons for asking.

There are a wide variety of methods for performing this kind of a divination. Any system which provides enough dynamism for a spirit to easily manipulate the process can be used. Dice rolls, marbles in a bowl, pendulum dowsing, or so on can all work for this. Pendulum dowsing is perhaps the most direct method but also the most susceptible to operator error in the form of inserting our own answers. It is generally best to have at least two tools available for use in divination, so that the methods can be checked against each other. Inconsistencies should be explored to determine if the spirit is having a difficult time of things, doesn't know the answers clearly, or simply is not participating.

All of these divination techniques assume we do not have specialized equipment on hand, and instead use materials easily available to most people. If you have specialized equipment for paranormal investigation, then these may be better options. They're far less *psychic* and it's somewhat less likely the spirit will understand how to work them, but they often deliver a higher degree of flexibility in answers. Most of these techniques are somewhat limited to simple answers. More sophisticated conversational answers can be obtained by channeling or telepathic communication.

Framing the Question

Before discussing individual divination techniques, it's prudent to discuss the framing of questions. Communication with spirits is always at best a fairly dicey prospect. Having them physically anchored in an abode is helpful, but even this doesn't ensure clear communication. As many spirits communicate more telepathically than verbally, the clarity of the question in our own mind is important. Short, direct questions with clear answers are ideal. It is also important to not ask questions with too many potential answers. Open ended questions are going to be difficult to divine, and are more likely to be successfully answered through channeling or mediumship.

The questions we want answered through divination should be yes or no, or have clear and distinct multiple choices. A good question would be "is it going to rain tomorrow," or "have you always resided here?" An example of a bad question might be "when would be the best time for me to plant begonias," or "what kind of things cause you to be upset?" There are ways to frame the latter two questions more favorably, however. For example, you might ask "if I plant begonias next week, how will that go?" followed by "if I plant begonias this week, how will that go?" and so on. Or, you might ask "when I make coffee using the grinder, does that upset you?" and "when I burn the garbage, does that upset you?" These questions allow firm, unambiguous answers.

When we have conflicting answers, it indicates several things could be going wrong. First and most obvious is that there's not an adequate connection to the spirit, or that the spirit isn't answering. After all, all of the methods involved will give some answer simply because there's no way for thrown dice not to land on an answer. In this case, you may reassess whether or not the spirit is present. If it is present, ask clarifying questions to verify answers. It is often helpful, as with a lie detector test, to ask some softball question where the answer is already known, in order to check the quality of the contact. In the event that the quality is complete garbage, it is often best to postpone until later, closing the session and letting the spirit go. Then more offerings can be made before inviting them again. If the responses are good, then you can proceed with your actual questions. Though we are asking baselining questions like a lie detector test, it's important to note that the goal here is not to try to catch the spirit in a lie; merely to verify the sensitivity of our instruments. Don't treat it as trying to "catch" the spirit in anything.

Dice Reading

Thrown dice are great for randomization in a way that spirits can influence. Ideally, the dice are rolled by cup rather than by hand, and turned directly down onto the table rather than thrown. Formulate the question, then state it clearly out loud. Repeating the question, roll the dice in the cup, and when you feel intuitively the time is right, turn the cup down on the table and lift it carefully so as not to disturb the dice.

There are a few options on how you would want to interpret answers. Assuming you are using a single 6-sided die, you could choose odds for "yes," evens for "no." Alternatively you could use upper numbers for "yes" and smaller numbers for "no." You might consider reducing the 6-sided die to 3 outcomes by subtracting 3 from the total if the number is greater than 3, so one and four are one, two and five are two, and three and six are three. This method allows for questions about potential future outcomes, for example, "good," "bad," or "mixed." Dice also lend themselves well towards ranked order responses. You may also consider rolling two dice together and checking for correspondent answers when using "yes" or "no" questions. Answers that oppose one another (one and four, for example) can be taken as ambiguity and prompt for repeating the question. Alternatively this can be used for "good," "bad," and "mixed" potential outcomes as well.

Another variation uses three dice and looks at odds and evens. Here the number of odds or evens indicates certainty. If odds are "no" and evens are "yes," then three evens would be very certain, two odds would be probably no, and so on.

What cannot be done is combinations of dice with numbers being added up. We should not use two dice on their own, for example, as the results are normally distributed and not intuitively. It would be unfortunate to have results of a divination skewed because statistics weighs too heavily against the spirit's ability to respond.

Marbles in a Bowl

With marbles in a bowl, the spirit influences the marbles as they spin about the bowl. Each marble has been assigned an answer value, and whichever exits the bowl first is the answer. Using multiple colored marbles placed in a regular bowl or chalice with an open even top, firmly and clearly identify what marble signifies what outcome. It may be useful to make sure the person spinning the bowl does not know the assignments of the numbers, to mitigate unconscious influence. Accomplishing this requires two people, of course: one to assign the answers to dice, and the other to spin the bowl.

As before, state the question directly. Then, picking up the bowl or cup and spinning it, repeat the question. Continue spinning the bowl until one of the marbles pops out. Whatever marble pops out is your answer. As usual, this works best with yes or no, good or bad, closed ended type questions. For shorter sessions, you can write out full statements for each marble, rather than a simple yes or no. This also has the benefit of allowing us to fully formulate and flesh out the exact phrasing we're aiming for. By writing out the possible answers each time we ask a question, we can get slightly more clarity than ambiguous "yes," or "no," but without muddying the waters through complicated open ended phrasings. Of course, if our phrases are not clear, or our options are not actual, any result we get may be wrong.

Pendulum Dowsing

Pendulum dowsing (or pendling) has its origins as a method of dowsing for water or other buried resources using maps, but can also be used to ask questions to spirits, or to ourselves, in order to discover information we're not consciously aware of. To pendulum dowse, we need a piece of paper and pen, or a pre-printed dowsing circle, and a pendulum of some sort. The pendulum can be anything so long as it can swing freely without kinking or otherwise having its arc disrupted. A string with a nut tied to one end is a good option, while an amulet on the end of a chain necklace is not, as chain

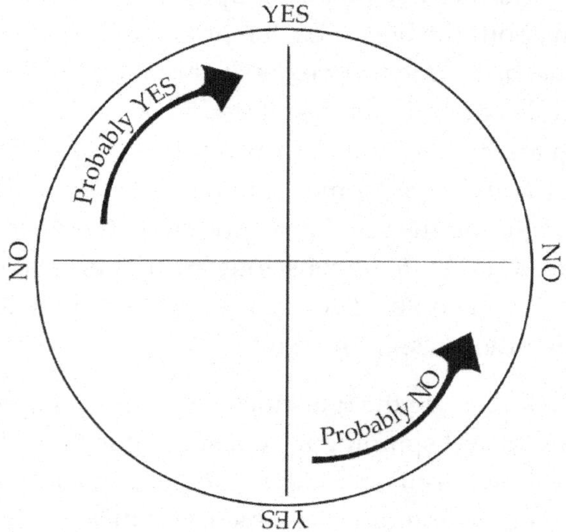

Figure 4 (A Simple Pendling Map)

can kink and necklaces favor swinging in certain directions. It can be as elaborate or as simple as you like.

When pendling, we mark on the paper directions for the pendulum to swing. At its most simple, swinging to and fro may mean yes, and side to side could mean no. We can also set meanings for circles, either clockwise or counterclockwise. This would make the most basic form of pendling circle. More sophisticated pendling circles may include the letters of the alphabet, but while this *seems* very liberating and able to provide open-ended answers, I will say that such is not practically the case. The length of time it takes to deliver an open ended response to a question, spelled letter by letter, is much longer than the time it takes to ask multiple clarifying questions. Beyond that, spirits are sometimes bad at spelling. Again, most spirits communicate telepathically, not verbally, so even phonetic spelling may be difficult. It is, of course, possible that we ourselves being the operators of the pendulum can do the work of spelling a concept unconsciously, but even this is less viable and more time consuming than simply asking a few yes or no questions to get the same amount of information.

There is also the problem of "resetting" the pendulum. Unless we have a very cooperative and somewhat powerfully psychokinetic spirit we're working with, the pendulum will maintain its momentum, so shifting from one letter to the next can introduce quite a bit of circular rotation after a few letters. It is therefore necessary to let the pendulum come to rest between letters. What may be a much quicker process of spelling is significantly slowed by this requirement and so I'm of the opinion it's best to keep the pendling circle simple and stick to forced response questions. We can leave open ended communications to more direct channeling and mediumship.

One notable reason we might use an alphabetic pendling field, however, would be to get a name for the spirit. This can also be done via channeling or mediumship, otherwise, pendulum dowsing remains one of the better ways to ask a spirit what it would like to be called, or how it can be called. Learning a name is not quite so dramatic as we'd think from fiction, but having a spirit's name does give us the ability to contact and work with that spirit at our own pleasure, and to make sure we're getting the same spirit. It's something equivalent to having a spirit's cell phone number. There's a degree of trust involved on the part of the spirit, and it shouldn't be taken lightly. In any case, having the spirit give us a name or sign or symbol which it can be called is one of the first divinatory operations we should perform, as this allows us to tailor future work towards that specific spirit, rather than vague and general pronouncements about "any local spirits." It is only with the name that we can establish with some accuracy with whom we have cultivated the relationship, and it is necessary for further work.

To actually pendle, hold the pendulum in the center of the circle on the paper on which you have marked your answers and directions, resting your elbow on the table and holding the string between the forefinger and thumb. "Calibrate" the pendulum by swinging it along the answer paths you want, forward and backward for "yes," for example, and side to side for "no," clockwise for "probably yes," counterclockwise for "probably no," for example. Once you have calibrated it, allow it to come to rest again. Once it is fully stationary, still holding it as before, state the question, repeating it as necessary if there is no response, until there is a very visible and solid response. Then, thank the spirit and allow it to come to rest again, repeating the process as desired.

It should be noted here that pendulum dowsing can work either through the psychokinetic influence of the spirit or through the telepathic influence of the spirit communicating through use of your own autonomic nervous system, where fine muscle movements in the fingers, almost imperceptible, bring about the effect. The latter is more common, and it is also in this way that pendling can be used to query our own unconscious mind or to perform a kind of "pure" divination, without an external spirit influence. The process remains generally the same, except that the question is asked generally instead of being directed towards a spirit.

Candle Questioning

Candle questioning is a very simple technique for asking very simple questions. In order to engage in a candle questioning session, first set up one or more candles in the working space in front of you. If you have conjured the spirit inside a circle, set the candles up inside the circle. You can use one candle or several. If you use more than one, arrange them how you please. For gravitas and in accordance with various other traditions, arranging them around the points of a pentacle is often good, as well as one in the center, making six candles. Alternatively, you may set five candles, with one in the center and one at each cardinal point; or nine candles, including cardinal and ordinal directions. However many you use, set them distant enough that they would not all be affected by the same ambient air pattern (such as your own breathing or movement) and set them far enough away from you to mitigate this concern as well.

Having conjured the spirit, you can go about asking it questions as in the divination procedures mentioned earlier in the book. These questions can be phrased in a few different ways. The most straightforward is the "yes or no" question format. What we're aiming for is for candles to flicker. When using yes or no questions, a good practice is to use "one flicker" for "no" and "flicker many times" for "yes." Some people will advocate for "flicker once for yes, twice for no" but I find that a continuous flickering is easier to identify than twice exactly and also easier for the spirit to achieve. A single flicker is also fairly obvious. When using multiple candles with yes or no, you should watch the entire field of candles. If all of them go, then this is a more confident or certain answer than if only a single one goes at once.

When asking things more specifically than yes or no questions, you can use directions to define multiple choices for selection, as with the different directions in pendulum dowsing. This can be accomplished by either defining them in part of the questions, or defining them as answers in a multiple choice series. The center candle can serve as a general "I don't know" or "cannot say" answer. Done this way, of course, if more than one candle responds then the answer will be unclear and will need clarification.

After any of the above divination practices are finished, it is best to thank the spirit for its cooperation and dismiss it. Generally, it is best to keep such divination sessions limited to just a few questions. Too many questions can exhaust the spirit as it exerts influence onto the system to bring about the answer, and it can exhaust us as we maintain contact, though not so much as mediumship would. If we have a good relationship with a spirit, it will often be possible to perform these divinations without preliminary rituals. However, this relationship should be established long before we attempt such a thing. Otherwise, as always, it is best to make offerings and so on beforehand.

Conducting a Session

Actually conducting a session is relatively simple once the essential skills have been mastered. How we go about it does not really change whether we are attempting to contact and communicate with our own local spirits or if we've been called in for consultation. There are some specific considerations for both, but the core remains the same.

Fundamentally, we want to create an atmosphere conducive to psychic working. This means ideally we should be undistracted and without environmental factors that could distract us. If a spirit makes itself known, this will be distracting enough on its own, so we don't need additional confounding factors (strobe lights, for example). We should attempt to maximize our own performance by having a healthy diet. It helps to abstain from meat or eggs on days when conducting a séance, because some spirits can smell those things on us and do not care for them. We should also consider avoiding offensive and strong foods like onion or garlic on those days. These are not strict rules (some spirits appreciate those things, after all), but can help when planning generally. Grounding, centering, and meditating prior to the séance helps put us in a receptive state of mind.

Trance mediums will want to make the room you'll be working in most closely resemble the circumstances they need. Edgar Cayce, for example, would lay on his back on a sofa with his shoes off and his hands folded in his lap. When invited to J.B. Rhine's laboratory for psychic testing, he declined because it would not have been an environment conducive to his talent functioning. Of course, if you are working for others it's sometimes necessary to go to the house, so exact circumstances can't be replicated. Still, having a place to lay down if the trance medium usually lays down is something you'd want. If the medium usually sits, he or she should have access to a seat, and so on. The more familiar the trance medium feels the situation is, the easier it will be to achieve the appropriate level of trance.

It's also best to avoid disturbing the home as much as possible. If a decision must be made between accommodating the medium and rearranging the house, accommodate the medium; but if a house is being haunted then we don't want to change too many variables.

If we're engaging in a séance as part of a paranormal investigation, then we need to also make sure that the medium isn't given too much information in advance. Ghost hunting shows on television make a big show of this to demonstrate the veracity of the medium, but it's more important to protect the medium from information that will make it harder to interpret communications. If there are pictures of a little girl all through a room, or if a room obviously belongs to a little girl, then a medium may have a hard time understanding if a spirit is talking about someone else. We want to insulate the medium from information that could potentially flavor the information as it comes in.

If we're using something like talking boards or automatic writing, we need to make sure that those can be set up well also. For instance, an automatic writer will need a desk and chair. It is difficult for an automatic writer to manage pen pressure, which makes it impossible to use a clipboard. Without a surface to write on, we're asking a bit too much of the medium. Similarly, when using a talking board, we must have a way to situate it so that everyone who will be involved is an equal distance from the planchette and the center of the board. If people's reach is uneven then the nearer person will have greater mechanical leverage over the planchette and the outcome can be biased.

The setting is a matter of some controversy. Strictly speaking, no special arrangements need to be made to the ambience of a room. We don't need to light candles, dim the lights, or so on. This has gone through some iterations over time. It's true that we can create conditions conducive to an experience if we light candles, set the lights dim, and so on. However, in the early 1900s, as fraudulent mediums were becoming more common, this became a cover for concealing the techniques being used. It is unfortunate that these same conditions conducive to trance and to a heightened state of alertness useful for observing paranormal phenomena.

But nothing about lighting candles, dimming lights, or waiting until midnight actually benefits the process of contacting spirits. There is nothing special about these circumstances that increase psychic performance. Clairvoyant gazing using specula can require dim conditions, but not in order to function. Rather, it's necessary the specula be dark and void so the psychic can project imagery into it, and a dim room helps for this.

The actual performance of psychic ability or communication with spirits benefits only inasmuch as these conditions tend to make us more alert. The darkness activates primal instincts that put us on edge. The flickering of candle lights creates movement that we instinctively attend to, watching for threats that might lurk out of sight. With this heightened state of alertness, we are more prepared to notice unexplained phenomena as they occur. Additionally, these conditions tap deeply into our cultural memory and prime us with the idea that we are in a psychic space. We use our culture's symbolism to indicate to our minds our purpose for being there. This creation of an atmosphere can help us in fulfilling our purpose, even while paranormal investigators are using sophisticated machinery to try to detect evidence. Replicating the mind's images of what a séance looks like helps us perform a séance, even though these conditions are not strictly necessary.

The actual session has a natural progression that is fairly familiar to anyone who has ever thrown a party. In the past, a séance would have been entertainment for a party, so this makes sense. After we've made the preparations, we should invite the guests, both spiritual and physical. Set up any necessary equipment, beginning with investigative tools like electronic voice recorders, and then proceeding to any tools that will be used for communication or divination. We begin with the recording devices in case of a spontaneous manifestation when the divination material is presented, as some spirits—especially those eager to talk to someone—will notice and begin at once. Light whatever candles and establish whatever ambience or atmosphere you prefer.

After all of the equipment is in place, arrange offerings and actually offer them. You can do this by simply speaking aloud your intent to offer those things once they are in place, and any conditions you would put on accepting the offerings or specific spirits you're attempting to contact. This is the invitation, and it's meant to attract the attention of spirits. Give some time for the spirits to enjoy the offerings.

After inviting the spirit, we want to make contact. State this intent firmly and out loud. If you have developed the skills earlier in the book, it can also help to project this intent. You'll want to be clear about the reason for contact, whether it is to hear what the spirit has to say, to make requests, or even just entertainment. We may ask the spirit to give us some kind of sign of its presence. This can be via flickering candles, interacting with our sensing equipment, or however the spirit chooses.

In some cases, we may want to give the spirit an object it can use as a temporary anchor in the physical world. I will often provide an array of such anchors, called *abodes*, to give a spirit a selection. These different abodes have different classical elemental compositions, allowing the spirit to choose that which with it is most sympathetic. When a spirit has chosen an abode, it will take on a draw or attraction, and it will be easily detected through psychometry. The abode gives the spirit a firm tether to the physical world which can help in etheric interactions and which can keep the spirit stable in the event of an unstable energetic environment, thus giving it more resources to use.

Once the spirit is confirmed present, we can get down to the actual work. If we are trying to divine information based on what the spirit knows, we should inform the spirit and then ask the first question, and follow the process for whatever type of divination you're doing. If instead you are trying for a more free-form communication, then this is the point where you would enter into a mediumistic trance, establish telepathic contact, or so on.

Once the communication is finished, we also want to thank the spirit for its time and send it on politely. Sometimes, spirits will want to linger about. Occasionally, they'll want to keep the abode. In this case the next session should be to determine what the rules and expectations are. Once the spirit is satisfied, send it on its way. If a paranormal investigation is underway, you may continue monitoring for some time, or move on to the next room or area and look to establish contact with other spirits. Here it's important to note that spirits are not really spatially bound, and so it is entirely possible for the same spirit to be interacting with multiple places in a house at the same time. Additionally, land spirits are intractably connected with the land itself, and so can interact everywhere in their domain, all at once. It is not surprising, then, to get the same spirit; and it may be useful to ask this early on to save ourselves establishing contact with the same spirit again and again.

How you conduct a session will largely be a matter of personal preference, in the end, combining your own preferences with those of the spirits you are trying to contact for the best results. Your sessions are your own, and your method of conducting them should follow what works best for you.

Hauntings occur whether we have a particular method for a session or not. By providing a structure for the spirit to contact us, we can mitigate some of the negative aspects of hauntings. For most, the problem of hauntings is that they are not understood by the people experiencing them. The haunted person may not realize that a spirit merely wants to communicate, or they may be agitating the spirit through action or inaction without being aware of this at all. Through structured sessions, we can determine the actual cause of the haunting. We can provide a venue for the spirit to communicate its concerns in controlled circumstances. When we do this, we do not try to end the haunting by forcefully driving away the spirit. Instead, we aim to live harmoniously with the spirits and to help others to do so as well. We achieve a harmonious haunting.

Further Reading

Auerbach, L. (1986). *ESP, hauntings and poltergeists: a parapsychologist's handbook.* New York: Warner Books.

Broughton, R.S. (1991). *Parapsychology: the controversial science.* New York, NY: Ballantine Books.

Butler, W.E. (1998). *How to read the aura: And practice psychometry, telepathy, & clairvoyance.* Rochester, VT: Destiny Books.

Leadbeater, C.W. (2009). *The chakras.* Anand Gholap Theosophical Institute.

Kardec, A. (1970). *The book on mediums: Guide for mediums and invocators.* Weiser.

Michaharic, D. (2012).

Mishlove, J. (1988). *PSI development systems.* New York, NY: Ballantine Books

Miller, J. (2006). *Protection and reversal magick.* Franklin Lakes, NJ: Red Wheel Weiser.

Miller, K. (2019). *Subtle energy: A handbook of psychic energy manipulation.* Frederick, MD: Turtles & Crows.

Miller, R.M., & Harper, J.M. (1986). *The psychic energy workbook.* New York, NY: Sterling Pub. Co.

Museum of Talking Boards. (n.d.). https://museumoftalkingboards.com

Naparstek, B. (1998). *Your sixth sense: Unlocking the power of your intuition.* New York: Harper One.

Steiner, R. (1909). *Initiation and its results.*

Stevenson, I. (1970). *Telepathic impressions: A review and report of 35 new cases.* Charlottesville, VA: University Press of Virginia.

Tamphel, K., Trans. (2010). Shamatha to mahamudra. New Delhi, India: Archana Press.

Vaughan, F.E. (1979). *Awakening intuition*. New York: Anchor Books.

About the Author

Keith Miller is a psychic and a lifelong student of the paranormal. He holds a master's degree in transpersonal psychology from Atlantic University. In addition to parapsychology and the paranormal, he has studied a wide range of occult topics, including Western and Tibetan astrology, divination, card reading, and radionics.

The author of several books on paranormal topics, Keith is also a teacher and lecturer. By studying methods of psi development from around the world, he has developed a systematic, step-by-step method of psychic ability development.

Made in the USA
Middletown, DE
03 February 2020